The Pat Browne Jr. Story

The

Pat Browne Jr.

Story

A Life Played Well

JIM FRAISER

PELICAN PUBLISHING
NEW ORLEANS

Library of Congress Cataloging-in-Publication Data

Names: Fraiser, Jim, 1954- author.
Title: The Pat Browne Jr. story : a life played well / Jim Fraiser.
Description: New Orleans, LA : Pelican Publishing, [2023] | Includes
index. | Summary: "Pat Browne Jr. was a star athlete at Jesuit High
School and Tulane University in New Orleans who became an attorney.
An All-American golfer, he was blinded in a car accident. He would
go on to win twenty-three blind pro golf tournaments. Arnold Palmer
nominated him for the World Golf Hall of Fame. This is his story" —
Provided by publisher.

Identifiers: LCCN 2022060634 | ISBN 9781455626885 (hardback : acid-free
paper) | ISBN 9781455626892 (ebook)
Subjects: LCSH: Browne, Patrick J., Jr. | Golfers—United States—
Biography. | Blind athletes—United States—Biography. | Golf for
people with disabilities—United States. | PGA World Golf Hall of
Fame. | Lawyers—United States—Biography. | Bankers—United
States—Biography. | BISAC: BIOGRAPHY & AUTOBIOGRAPHY /
Sports
Classification: LCC GV964.B76 A3 2023 | DDC 796.352092 [B]—dc23/
eng/20230210
LC record available at https://lccn.loc.gov/2022060634

All photographs courtesy of Pat Browne Jr., his family, and friends

Printed in the United States of America
Published by Pelican Publishing
New Orleans, LA
www.pelicanpub.com

*In memory of my daughter Luci
and for Paul, Mary Adelyn, and Corinne*

Character cannot be developed in ease and quiet. Only through experience of trial and suffering can the soul be strengthened, vision cleared, ambition inspired, and success achieved.

—Helen Keller

I say, don't quit. Suffer now and live the rest of your life as a champion. But don't forget — service to others is the rent you pay for your room in Heaven.

—Muhammad Ali

CONTENTS

PREFACE

Sometimes God brings times of transition to create transformations.

—Lynn Cowell

Obstacles and setbacks are inevitable. How you respond to them will determine if you have what it takes to meet challenges and become a champion.

—Germany Kent

The year 1966 would prove a momentous one in many different ways, for better and for worse. Sandwiched between the Korean War and the ongoing conflict in Vietnam and shifting between the staid perspectives of the Greatest Generation and the progressive views of those committed to social change, the year would stand out as a time of transition for many.

America would see Walt Disney die and Troy Aikman born. Bobbie Gibb would become the first woman to enter the Boston Marathon, while slugger Frank Robinson would win Major League Baseball's coveted Triple Crown. An artificial heart would be installed in a man's chest, and the St. Louis Arch would be dedicated. The *Star Trek* television series would launch, as would *It's The Great Pumpkin, Charlie Brown*. Bob Dylan would be injured in a motorcycle accident near Woodstock, New York, and New York City would witness the groundbreaking

9

of the World Trade Center. The Beatles would give their last concert as a touring band and "It's a Small World" would open at Disneyland. Stevie Wonder, and another blind singer, Ray Charles, debuted not one but two R&B albums each.

Closer to the center of gravity of this story, the National Football League would award a franchise to the city of New Orleans. An amendment to the Louisiana state constitution would allow governors to succeed themselves for a second term, and John McKeithen would be the first to earn that opportunity. Victor H. Schiro served that year as mayor of New Orleans, while a future, more colorful governor, Moon Landrieu, would take a seat on the city council.

The Tulane Green Wave football team, finishing with a record of 5-4-1 in 1966, would play its last Southeastern Conference football game against LSU, losing 21-7. But another sport would see a strange and tragic beginning of sorts near New Orleans, Louisiana on February 17, 1966. The sport, a unique variation of professional golf, was not born in 1966; rather its beginnings hailed back to the 1930s.

But the man who would become that game's greatest champion was reborn in 1966—a birthing in the truest sense of blood and pain. It was a beginning that would ultimately yield perhaps one of the most unbelievable stories New Orleans would ever know. One so incredible as to make most people today, upon hearing it, ask if it were really true, or just like another episode of the rebooted 1960s TV series, *The Twilight Zone*.

Yet this is a true story—the Pat Browne Jr. story—and that story begins right now.

Acknowledgments

When New Orleanian Dick Meyers brought this incredible story to me, suggesting that I pen a biography of Pat Browne Jr. — the lawyer who was blinded and became the greatest blind golfer of all time — I thought he was suggesting a novel. How could such a thing really be true?

But that was only a part of this story. Even more extraordinary was what an amazing man Pat was — a splendid multi-sport all-star athlete, an accomplished lawyer and bank CEO for decades after becoming sightless, and a loving family man and loyal friend loved and admired by all who knew him.

This is a sports book, yes, but it's also a book about a real life hero, one eulogized by a good friend as "the greatest man who ever lived." Pat was a man who refused to let terrible blows knock him down. He got back up after being robbed of his sight to make a second life for himself. And a major part of that life was giving back to others — raising millions of dollars for those who had suffered blindness and other difficulties in their lives.

I am grateful to Pat's wife, Sherry, and his son, Patrick, who gifted me this wonderful story, and to Pat's many family members, colleagues, and friends who opened their hearts to me about the man they loved and respected as much as any they had ever known.

The

Pat
Browne
Jr.
Story

1

A Louisiana Odyssey Begins with Loss

To succeed in life, one must have determination and must be prepared to suffer during the process, or I don't see how he can really be successful.

—Gary Player

The ideal man bears the accidents of life with dignity and grace, making the best of circumstances.

—Aristotle

Winters in the Deep South can often be chilly. This is due more to the wetness than the temperature, but rarely cold enough to warrant gloves, a scarf and a complete wool outfit. Such was the case on February 17, 1966, a cloudy day with temperatures hovering in the high fifties to low sixties near New Orleans, Louisiana. Pat Browne Jr., a New Orleans lawyer with the firm of Jones Walker, LLP since graduating from Tulane Law School in 1959, was riding back to his hometown of New Orleans in a car driven by his cousin and fellow lawyer Bill Kyle. They were returning from an early afternoon wedding in Baton Rouge, and the conversation had at first been as light and breezy as the day.

The sun still shone, but now only weakly through a cloud-flecked winter sky. Traffic was sparse coming and going on the two-lane Airline Highway they were traversing. This gave Bill and Pat an abundance of time to converse, but after thirty minutes passed, Bill noticed that the usually gregarious Pat seemed uncommonly distant, even pensive to a fault. Or had a touch of sadness crossed Pat's visage before he turned away to gaze out the front passenger side window?

"Something eating you, Pat?" Bill asked. "I don't mean to pry, but you don't seem your usual jovial self. You haven't joked about my driving since we left the wedding in Baton Rouge. You worried our cousin made a bad match?"

Then Bill noticed, or thought he did, that Pat had winced slightly on hearing his remark about the wedding.

"No Bill, I'm fine," Pat smiled wanly. "How could I not be? A lovely wedding and a smooth ride back home, except for you having almost killed us outside Gonzales, and we're only halfway home."

"Now that's the Pat Browne I know! But hey, you're almost safe. We're closer to home than you think. Good Hope Community is just up ahead. We're not that far from Ochsner Hospital in Metairie and even closer to the New Orleans Airport, where you should have gone if you didn't like my driving."

Bill watched Pat closely until the latter gave a broad smile in response. For a fleeting moment Bill thought he saw the familiar sparkle in Pat's eyes that showed through even the darkest sunglasses.

"Now that's the spirit, Pat. Like you say, how could you not be happy, after all? You're a partner in a great law firm, two strokes from being a scratch golfer. . . . "

"I'm not quite that good, Bill. Hell, you putt better than I do."

"No," Bill chuckled. "Don't get humble on me now.

You lettered at golf and basketball at Tulane, were a star baseball player in high school at Jesuit, won the damn World Series there, and you've only gotten better on the links every year. Oh, I could probably take you in basketball now."

"Sure you could. With me blind in one eye with one leg in a cast, you might even score on me. Once."

After sharing a warm smile with his cousin and law partner, Pat grew silent once more, his chin resting on a thumb and finger, his eyes fixed on the bare willow oaks and nuttall oaks passing by outside his window. Bill's lawyerly instincts told him that something was up, so he decided to pursue a different line of questioning.

"Maybe I could score on you, Pat, but any deficiency on my part would be because you stand six four while I'm decidedly shorter. But one thing's for sure, you've outscored almost everybody in the family department. You're married to a beautiful wife who gave you three lovely daughters. It doesn't get any better than that, eh? Winning at golf, winning in the courtroom, and things only get better when you get back to your wife and kids."

Like a witness who sees his case slipping away on the witness stand, Pat gave a noticeable sigh and turned to face his friendly interlocutor. This time he didn't even attempt to force a weak smile. "I've told no one this, Bill, and I apologize for burdening you with it, but it's really getting to me and I need to talk to someone about it."

"Sure, Pat. You know you can talk to me about anything. Now or over a few drinks at the club, your call."

"Bill, just between you and me, I don't think my marriage is going to last. It's nobody's fault, really, we just don't get along, no matter how hard I try. And."

Bill waited for his companion to continue. He certainly hadn't expected anything like this, but Pat Browne Jr. had 'held his hand' so to speak, many times on the golf course or in his law office when trouble had sought him out, and the least he could do was offer a consoling ear.

Pat cleared his throat then looked straight ahead before he continued speaking in somber tones. "I'm afraid she's going to leave me, Bill, and take my three daughters to Tampa, Florida where she grew up. She's wanted to live there for many years. I won't know what to do if . . . "

Pat froze in mid-sentence. "Bill!" he shouted, pointing frantically outside the front glass. But his warning came too late. From the other side of the two-lane highway, the lane with traffic headed toward Baton Rouge, a car had bounced across the neutral ground between the lanes and barreled headlong towards them at fifty miles an hour.

A driver, sotted with whiskey, lost control of his stolen car and forced a collision that took his own life. But no one knew that at the time.

Pat fared only slightly better. Bill suffered a broken arm and fractured skull, but Pat's injuries were catastrophic. When the drunk driver's car hit Bill's vehicle head on, it drove Bill's car hood directly into Pat's face and eyes.

Pat heard the terrible sound of metal tearing through metal, and the last thing he would ever see was a flashing blue light shortly after the hood struck him, shattering his face, crushing his nose, breaking multiple bones, and blinding him forever.

2

THE FAITH OF A MODERN-DAY JOB

God is faithful, and he will not let you be tested beyond your strength. He will also provide the way out so you may be able to endure it.

—1 Corinthians 10:13

Kindness is a language which the deaf can hear and the blind can see.

—Christian Nestell Bovee

Pat awoke in a bed in Ochsner Hospital in Metairie, Louisiana, shrouded in total darkness. He faced numerous surgeries to repair the damage to his face, fractured leg and head, but his optic nerve had been severed and no surgery could ever recover his lost eyesight.

This last news was delivered to Pat by Dr. Johnny Ochsner, a longtime friend who didn't recognize him when Pat went rolling by on a stretcher at the hospital entrance. Johnny was leaving for the day at that time and hadn't recognized Pat due to the terrible injuries to his face.

Upon hearing that the accident victim was his old friend, Dr. Ochsner hurried back to the hospital to take charge of Pat's treatment. He found Pat's head to be the size of a watermelon, his chest battered and his heartbeat barely discernible. But he stabilized his patient and before long there was only the question of how long a full recovery would take.

Physical recovery required twenty plastic surgeries to repair Pat's cheek bones and reroute his nose, ultimately leaving a blue scar on the nose's right side. His arms and legs required extensive treatment also, leaving him practically bed ridden for three months before he could move around in a semi-normal fashion.

His jaw was broken and he couldn't eat initially, causing him to become anemic. His weight soon fell from 210 pounds to 170. "But I went to Tulane and put myself in the hands of good old Bubba Porche—head athletic trainer for the Tulane University football team at the time—and he got me back up to 195," Pat would later recall, "and it was the best I ever felt in my life." He left the hospital after a four month stay.

Emotional recovery would prove a significantly greater challenge. As he had expected, his marriage did fail, and he and his wife divorced in 1967. She promptly took their three young daughters, Katherine, Shannon and Gay, almost a thousand miles away to her Tampa hometown.

Many people may have been daunted by such terrible strokes of fate, but not Pat Browne Jr. Thanks to his abundant faith in God and himself, his quiet confidence acquired by success in academics and sports, and his achievements in the practice of law, he never doubted for a moment that he would make a good life for himself despite being sightless.

"What made it easy for me," Pat would later say, "was the abundance of friends and, I guess, the things I learned as an athlete. Things like, if you're knocked down, get up."

But the road ahead was not without barriers. Pat was forced to move in with his parents, Dorothy and Pat Walsh Browne Sr., in Uptown New Orleans. They would be responsible for his hourly, day-to-day needs until he was back on his feet. Transportation was partly covered when he contracted with United Cab to take him to work, to the doctor, and to other needful places.

Whenever he needed to go out and relax with his friends, two of his law partners and fellow Uptown residents, Henry Sarpy and Donnie Doyle, and his old friend turned petroleum geologist, Richard "Pepe" Colomes, among others, would transport him or go with him for dinner or diversion. Deciding not to learn Braille, Pat chose instead to rely on family and friends to guide him through life. This would prove no imposition on them, as they had all loved and admired Pat his entire life, for reasons that will soon become evident.

When he returned to his law firm seven months after the accident, his able secretary, Natalie Jones, read all the necessary papers to him and typed his letters, briefs and other court documents. Ironically, despite the terrible car wreck he suffered, Pat primarily represented Hertz and Avis as lead counsel.

One of his first cases upon his return to Jones Walker led to the defense of an unwinnable case in October of 1966. He represented a company whose forklift truck driver had run into the back of a taxi, seriously injuring a back seat passenger who required nine costly operations to return to decent health. The jury returned a $130,000 judgment against his client, prompting Pat to later proclaim, "That was some comeback."

And there were other bumps in that road too. In another case, in which he ultimately prevailed, he got turned around attempting to give a closing argument to the judge, and began speaking to the wall before his co-

counsel got him turned in the right direction. On another occasion, while appearing before the Louisiana Supreme Court, one of the Justices berated him for wearing his sunglasses in the courtroom.

When Pat stood to speak, the offended judge said, "Excuse me sir, but do you know you're addressing the Louisiana Supreme Court? Your outlandish playboy sunglasses are an insult to this court!"

This judge continued blasting Pat for several minutes for his supposed failure to comply with time-honored courtroom decorum until another justice elbowed him a second time and whispered, "Shut up, you ass. That's Pat Browne and he's blind." Shaken to his core, the now humbled adjudicator apologized and allowed Pat to continue his argument.

Yet Pat would remain a very successful trial lawyer with Jones Walker until he retired from the firm in 1979 to become president and CEO of one of his former clients, the Hibernia Homestead Bank. He would remain in that post for another incredible thirty years.

He never considered his professional accomplishments an act of courage, but rather a consequence of good fortune. "I could have been a cab driver or a doctor," Pat later recalled. "If I had, the transition would have been awfully tough. But I was a lawyer, a job in which hearing and speech is more important than sight."

Even so, Pat had suffered two major blows that would have destroyed a less determined man — a car wreck that crushed his bones and took his sight, and a divorce a year later that separated him from his children by almost a thousand miles.

According to his friend Pepe Colomes, it took Pat about

two years to emotionally "come to grips with it all." He did so, Pepe recalls, in large part due to his inexhaustible faith. Having been reared by very religious parents, and having matriculated at Jesuit High School, as well as attending Holy Name of Jesus Catholic Church near Tulane University in Uptown New Orleans, Pat had the "impetus to overcome his problems and never give up."

"Pat never complained about the accident or anything else," Pepe remembered. "And he never failed to fly to Tampa to see his little girls, renting a hotel room and seeing them when they came to visit. He always said, 'I'll do my best and remember that God loves me and will find a way to get me through it.' He had a motto, I believe, based on a passage in the Bible that went something like 'God never puts more on a person than they can handle.' I believe that, along with his high IQ and his natural athletic ability, he never doubted that he would succeed in anything he attempted after the accident.

"In fact," Pepe continued, "Pat joked about the accident and his blindness all the time. Sometimes, when we were sitting around with nothing to do, we would roll dice, and he was very lucky at that game. Somebody would say something like, you're a cruel SOB to keep winning like that. If nobody said something of that kind, he would ask us what was wrong."

Pat's daughter, Gay Browne Hardy, remembered how well he took his difficulties. "I was so young when dad had his accident that I don't really remember him having sight. I only recall him as being sightless," she said. "Even so, I never thought of him as being different from other fathers or handicapped in any way. He could do everything I needed him to do, he just did it wearing those sunglasses in the house. I never felt like he had obstacles to overcome. He never complained about anything and he could recognize everyone by their voices even from far away.

"Dad had a great memory and could retain so much. And there was never a hint of poor pitiful me. He used his golf club as a cane, giving even less of a hint of being handicapped. He went out the door every day and got back to life. He would walk down the street with his hand on my shoulder with no problem at all. And when we rode the streetcar in New Orleans he remembered what all the houses (on St. Charles Avenue) looked like when he spoke to me about them. He used Yellow Cab so much that he was probably the first person in New Orleans to have an account with a taxi company.

"He lived life fully," Gay recalled, "by the grace of God and with Sherry and his friends to take him where he needed to go. Dad was a committed father who came to see me and my sisters in Tampa once a month, no matter what. He did everything he possibly could for us. He had so much wisdom, and was so approachable, with such a positive attitude, that he could help us solve our problems without us ever even realizing it at the time. I really loved my dad."

Family and friendship would prove more than just a solace to Pat at this key juncture in his life. It would lead him to his greatest accomplishments as an athlete, and to achieving the love and admiration of people around the world.

3

The Comeback Trail

A journey of a thousand miles begins with a single step.
—Lao Tzu

Although Pat continued his early 1970s successes as a civil defense attorney, entertained good relations with his family and friends, and ultimately relegated the accident that blinded him to the past, he soon became aware of an emerging goal in his life. As a former Hall of Fame athlete in high school and college, he felt he should achieve something great in sport, but there was that little problem of blindness standing in his way. His only possibility was golf, but . . .

Enter Pepe Colomes, Henry Sarpy, and Donnie Doyle, who urged him to learn about blind golf and take up that sport with their help. As Pat later said, "I simply couldn't hit the ball with an iron, but my coach gave me a wood, and after I struck the ball soundly with that club a few times, I was hooked on golf again."

An avid researcher as a law student and practicing attorney, and now a fan of listening to books on record, tape and later CD, Pat began learning the history of blind golf in preparation of someday soon playing the game.

Blind golf, a sport unknown to many, had its beginnings in a challenge issued in 1938. *Ripley's Believe It or Not* had published two different stories—one in 1932 and another in 1938—about the world's "only" blind golfer. The articles named two different men in the articles: Minnesota's Clint Russell and England's Dr. Beach Oxenham. Russell's friends challenged Ripley to set up a Blind Golfer's Championship in August of 1938 at a country club in Duluth, Minnesota. Upon receiving contacts from other blind golfers, Clint Russell contacted the Veteran's Administration — a communique that eventually led to a 1946 national blind golfer's championship held in Inglewood, California. Charley Boswell, a future champion who had lost his sight during WWII, finished second.

In 1953, a blind golfer and Philadelphia lawyer established the United States Blind Golf Association, an organization that Pat Browne Jr. would come to serve as president from 1976 until 1992. Charley Boswell would win sixteen USBGA championships while Joe Lazaro, who also lost his sight in WWII, would win seven, but their records would later be eclipsed by Browne. But that is getting too far ahead in our story.

The USBGA championship was played on different courses until 1990, then at Lake Buena Vista Club at Disney World through 1997 thanks in part to the work and advocacy of Pat Browne Jr. Numerous celebrities would participate with the association, including Bob Hope, Prince Andrew, former President Gerald Ford, Archie Manning, and professional golfers Ian Baker-Finch and Payne Stewart. Other USBGA sanctioned championships would arise, including the Guiding Eyes Classic — dubbed the "Masters" of blind golf — that has been played in Mount Kisco, New York since 1978. Hosted by Ken Venturi for twenty-five years, and by Eli Manning since 2007, Guiding Eyes has raised well over ten million dollars for the training of guide dogs and instructions for their use, graduating over 8000 guide dogs in the process. But that situation, and Pat's involvement in it, would come much later.

All Pat knew in the late 1960s was that people did play golf despite blindness, and the sport was so popular that a national championship was established for its practitioners through the USBGA. Pat began entertaining a notion that he would someday win that championship, hopefully while his longtime idol, his father, was still alive.

Pepe Colomes made him work on his chipping, and helped him with his hooking drive, and taught him how to bump and run near the greens. Henry and Donnie worked with him when they could, and it wasn't long

Disney National Championship tournament, 1993, won by Pat and Gerry Barousse, with Mickey and Minnie

Disney World tournament with Payne Stewart and Worth Dalton, Mickey, and Minnie

before he had become "quite good" in their eyes. It only remained for his friends to master the technique of "coaching" him, or rather, guiding him to make his shots.

That process required Pat's coaches to position him in a stance with the ball, help him with club choice, distances to the hole or over obstacles, changes in fairway elevations, curving lines and lengths of putts. The coach would place one hand on the clubs' shaft and place the club head in position behind the ball. On the green Pat could walk from his lie to the hole to get a feeling of the length and curvature of the shot, a move that helped a great deal more than just having the coach rattle the cup when taking the pin out.

Ever the optimist, Pat claimed he had advantages over sighted golfers on the links. "I never look up," he was often heard to say, "and I never see the hazards." Nevertheless, he once quipped, "I lose a lot of money on Saturdays."

Blind golf tournaments offered other challenges that many duffers never faced. Their layouts were often more difficult than the usual country club or municipal courses, the roughs rougher and the greens like putting on glass. There was far better competition of course, but many times championship games were played in rain or on courses inundated before by storms and even hurricanes. Uphill and downhill lies presented risks of wild shots and even losing balance and falling down the hill. But perhaps the worst condition faced by blind golfers was the crowd noise, far more distracting to sightless golfers than to those with sight.

However blind golf official rules gave non-sighted golfers two advantages. They allowed them to ground their clubs in bunkers and hazards and allowed their coaches to remain standing in the direct line of the hole right behind them.

The stance and approach to the ball being very important, coaches would help align a player's shoulders and guide his club to a spot directly behind the ball. They would make sure his stance vis-a-vis the shot or putt was the correct one, then describe the path of this ball in flight or on the green similar to the way TV announcers did during televised tournaments, such as, "straight over a bunker with a wedge to middle of the green," or "hit it like a six-foot putt but due to the break."

After offering all the advice he can, the coach stands up, backs off, and says, "I'm out of the way," After the shot the coach might say, "That one was low and to the right," or "that putt fell two-feet short below the hole." The coach's knowledge and golfing abilities were a major factor in their ability to aid their charge's chances of winning.

"I was just a hacker, not a real golfer like Henry or Donnie," Pepe recalls, "but Pat never blamed me for a bad shot. It was always his fault. And he wanted it true; if his shot stunk, he wanted to hear it or he would have something rough to say about it, always in jest of course. He wanted to be treated like anyone else with two good eyes, to be just another one of the guys. We all respected that and gave him his due."

Pat greatly appreciated the help his good friends as coaches gave him. Pepe and Bobby Monsted during the early learning process, then others who were good enough to assist him during serious competition. As he would later say, "I owe everything to great friends — my dad, of course, and people like Henry Sarpy and Donnie Doyle. My job is easy. Henry and Don have the patience and they have to do all the bending and stooping."

So from 1967 to 1975, Pepe, Henry and Donnie, along with other friends as coaches such as Gerry Barousse, Jamie Christovich, David Clark, Charles Monsted and others, helped Pat prepare to face the two toughest challenges he would encounter during the next few decades. These would be playing other very talented blind golfers and overcoming blindness sufficiently to defeat those golfers in national championship tournaments. Those challenges would increase dramatically when he played tournaments on his home course before friends and family at the New Orleans Country Club.

4

FROM DARKNESS INTO LOVE'S SHINING LIGHT

The most important shot in golf is the next one.
— Ben Hogan

Resolve never to quit, never to give up, no matter the situation.
— Jack Nicklaus

When he wasn't practicing law, hitting balls on the golf range at the New Orleans Country Club with Henry Sarpy or Bobby Monsted, Pat enjoyed listening to books on record or tape. He particularly liked action thrillers, crime, mystery, and history books. The one he enjoyed the most, and that so greatly influenced his life, was champion blind golfer Charley Boswell's book, *Now I See.* Boswell had played football at the University of Alabama as well as minor league baseball for the Atlanta Crackers but had lost his sight pulling a fellow soldier out of a burning Sherman tank during World War II. Despite the fact that he had never played golf while sighted, he ultimately won sixteen USBGA National Championships between 1947 and 1970. From 1949 to 1961 he won them all, along with eleven international blind golf championships.

While forging a successful career as an independent insurance agent and later serving as Alabama Commissioner of Revenue for eight years, he worked with celebrity host Bob Hope to raise well over a million dollars during the fifteen years he hosted the Charley Boswell

Celebrity Classic supporting Birmingham's Eye Foundation Hospital.

During this time Pat also learned about the second greatest blind golfer, Joe Lazaro, who had been the eldest son of Sicilian immigrants and gone on to win seven USBGA championships and two international championships, despite having only been caddying and "fooling around with golf" as a teenager. Joe had lost his sight during WWII after landing at Salerno during the Italian offensive and encountering a land mine near Florence, Italy. During his career as a truck driver, Joe never forgot what the sport of blind golf had done for him, and launched the Lazaro Celebrity Hope for the Blind charity golf tournament in 1971. This Lion's Club-supported tournament raised thousands of dollars for charities in Massachusetts for over forty years, aided by celebrities such as Bob Hope. Joe had frequently entertained Arnold Palmer and Jack Nicklaus when they visited him in Boston.

Inspired and greatly impressed with the careers and charitable contributions made by Charley Boswell and Joe Lazaro, Pat became even more determined to make a similar mark on blind golf and to give back to others along the way. But the road ahead would be a long one, and always cloaked in darkness.

Practicing law while blind never proved a great challenge for him. Forging a second life for himself as a husband and father seemed a larger hill to climb. But taking on and overcoming the likes of Charley Boswell and Joe Lazaro in championship matches seemed the most impossible dream of all. Even so, Pat never doubted for a moment that he would achieve that goal.

Learning to play the game well with sight had been difficult enough. The best way for sighted golfers to understand the difficulties presented by blind golf is to put on a blindfold and try to hit a golf ball. As all golfers know, hitting one with full sight is difficult enough. Imagine hitting one long and straight and making precise chips and putts wearing that blindfold.

But the difficulty doesn't begin on the golf course. Try walking from the car to the clubhouse to get your clubs, then shuffling over to the practice tee without stubbing your toe or tripping over a step. You'll find that stroll to be most disconcerting, as is walking a course or stepping out of a golf cart to hit your ball!

Of course, none of that would even be possible without an unbelievable determination to succeed, and without patient and loyal coaches who were willing to sacrifice their time and suffer extensive impositions on their daily lives and take you to the club to practice, and later, to play several rounds every week.

After Bobby Monsted and Pepe Colomes had coaxed Pat into taking up blind golf and introduced him to the fundamentals of blind golf, Henry Sarpy took on the role of first coach and worked with Pat whenever he could.

For his part, Pat took to the training like the proverbial duck to water. "I had always loved the game," he often said, "and I thought it was worth taking a chance to see if I could hit it again. I wanted to know if I could do it again and [Henry and I] did it!"

When Henry could not spare the time for practice on a given day, Donnie Doyle filled in when his time allowed. But they all soon discovered that they could not simply go out and take turns coaching Pat. They realized they had to work out a system with Pat and stick to it every time any of them coached him.

But why would any young man sacrifice so much of his time to do this, as Henry and Donnie were now doing? The answer was because Pat was such a selfless, caring person who would himself always be there for others. He loved competition, and all his coaches knew that he would give his very best every outing and demand the same of his coaches. Much the same as did Jack Nicklaus, Pat out-worked everyone with his driving determination to some-day be the best blind golfer in the world. In fact, author and journalist Robert Sullivan would one day declare that "if Lazaro and Boswell were the Hogan and Palmer of blind golf, then Browne has been the Jack Nicklaus."

Pat was a born leader, a father figure to his young coaches who, with his sense of humor and never-say-die mentality, made the experience fun for his youthful friends. One of his later coaches, David Clark, came to Point Clear, Alabama from Kentucky, knowing no one in the area. Pat introduced him to friends in Point Clear, Alabama, where Pat often played, made David feel like a part of Pat's family, and later served as godfather to David's daughter. Another of his coaches, Jamie Christovich, was a young man that Pat had helped work on his golf game during his high school and college playing days.

Eventually, as Pat's game improved, Henry declared it was time for him to consider entering blind golf tournaments. He took Pat to listen to tournaments and helped him play golf in and around New Orleans.

As a *Times-Picayune* columnist noted in a 1971 article, Pat would attend tournaments and position himself near

The perfect swing of the greatest blind golfer of all time

the first tee. There "he would wait . . . and listen. From the sound of the club hitting the ball, Browne could tell instantly if the golfer had made solid contact."

By 1969, Pat was ready to enter blind golf tournaments, often invitational tournaments put on for various charities. In these matches, blind golfers were frequently paired with celebrities or professional golfers.

Pat's first USBGA national championship event took place in Chattanooga in 1969, a mere three years after he was blinded in an auto accident. There he and coach Pepe Colomes finished seventh, the winners being none other than Joe Lazaro and his coach John Callahan.

The next year Pat and his coach Henry Sarpy, his law partner of around the same age, participated in several events. In September at the Greensboro USBGA National Championship Tournament, a course pocked with rolling

hills, he shot 99-108 to finish third behind winner Charley Boswell and his coach Bo Russell, who shot 93-107.
Second-place finisher Joe Lazaro carded a 100-101.

There, Pat had been paired with 1957 PGA champion
and Ryder Cup participant Lionel Herbert in the Pro-Am
round. On the practice range the next day, Pat told *Times-
Picayune* journalist Peter Finney that, "Lionel couldn't
have been nicer. I was playing badly and he went out of
his way, telling me how to get more body turn into my
shots and how to take the club back."

Also in 1970, Pat scored his best round, an 83, in a
San Diego invitational established to raise funds for the
handicapped. His partner for that round was Dick Martin
of the popular *Rowan and Martin* TV show. He also met
Odd Couple star actor Jack Lemmon during the invitational.

He also played in a Pro-Am in Florida at Lakewood
International before entering the USBGA National
Championship tournament at Houston's H&H Guest
Ranch course in September of 1971.

While preparing for that event, he told Finney that,
"they tell me the course is flat, and that's good news. Those
hilly layouts always gave me trouble, even when I could
see the hills." Indeed, hilly courses had always presented
difficulties for Pat, who never entirely conquered uphill
and downhill lies.

Flat course or not, Pat couldn't get the win in Houston,
losing once again to the formidable Joe Lazaro and his
coach Steve Martini on a course drenched by rain courtesy
of Hurricane Fern. Lazaro had led Pat 89 to 93 on the first
day, and refused to give any ground on the second day.

If there was any silver lining in the "having to face Joe
Lazaro" dark cloud, it was the fact that he would no longer

Pat Browne Jr. with Jack Lemmon

be forced to face perennial champion Charley Boswell in his top form. Charley had won the USBGA championship more than any other golfer, including consecutively from 1949 to 1961. He would prevail for the last time in 1970, but continue playing the championships for several more years, where he would enjoy the respect and affection of everyone on and off the course.

Former Ole Miss All-American and New Orleans Saints All-Pro quarterback Archie Manning remembers a humorous event that occurred during his friendship with Charley Boswell.

"In 1971 I moved to New Orleans and joined the New Orleans Country Club in 1974. I was just taking up golf and met Pat there, and enjoyed playing with him very much," Archie related. During that time Manning had also met Charley Boswell during charity pro-am celebrity events at the club and in Birmingham where they first met. "At an event in the seventies hosted by the New Orleans Country Club, I hit balls with Charley and played against him in a Pro-Am celebrity tournament that featured Bob Hope, Joe Namath and Gerald Ford. Afterwards Charley invited me to speak to the Birmingham Touchdown Club, where he introduced me with a true story.

"We had exchanged tickets for a few years, him giving me tickets to big events and I getting him tickets to the Saints games. He ribbed me that one year after he had gotten me a ticket to a big game, I had gotten him, a

With President Gerald Ford while both playing in a celebrity tournament in New Orleans

former Crimson Tide football star, a ticket behind a pole during a Saints game."

Manning also recalled that Pat and Charley had become friends, even joking with each other on the course. "Once," Manning said, "they were playing on a par-4, hole number five, when Charley hit a funky shot." Pat told him, "That's the worst shot I've ever heard. But the fact is," Manning concluded, "Charley had a big impact on Pat."

Pat would shoot for the 1972 championship, his game now improved to the point that he felt worthy of the opportunity to face the likes of Charley Boswell and Joe Lazaro and any other challengers that might arise. But before that, Pat would enjoy one of the greatest successes of his life off the golf course.

For in 1972 Pat would find one of the most important influences on his life, and ultimately, his golfing career, far away from the links. In the spring of 1972 he met the woman he would eventually marry, albeit six years in the future.

He had tried dating only rarely to that point. A difficult marriage and painful divorce had taught him to be cautious, or perhaps overcautious, about making such a commitment ever again.

His friend and law partner Jerry Weigel recalled how one first date failed to inspire Pat to pursue a second. Although the prospect had no problem shepherding him around town, and had been a perfect lady just as Pat had been a perfect gentleman, there simply hadn't been any sparks or chemistry between them during Pat's weak efforts to make conversation. Fortunately they had double-dated with the Weigels so the conversation never lagged beyond repair.

The next day Pat phoned Jerry to discuss the event, and ended the conversation by asking, "By the way, how did she look?"

"I got bad news for you," Jerry laughed. "She looked like she had been in that accident with you."

Pat's luck improved dramatically when in February of 1972 he met a lovely 22-year old Sherry Shields. Born in Tampa, Florida, in 1943, she was eleven years his junior. They met on what she would later quip was a 'blind' date. At the time, Sherry taught at the Academy of Sacred Heart, an all-girls school, from 1st grade to the 12th, located on St. Charles Avenue in Uptown New Orleans. She had recently moved to the city from Tampa, where she had grown up, and had coincidentally lived in the same neighborhood as Pat's ex-wife. Sherry had been vaguely familiar with Pat's history, having heard about his car wreck and seen him in her neighborhood visiting his daughters.

"But I hadn't realized," Sherry recalled, "that he was blind. He never carried himself like he was handicapped in any way, so I thought the sunglasses were because he had very light colored eyes and was bothered by the Tampa sun."

Indeed, this was frequently the case with many who only had passing acquaintance with Pat. Metairie resident and fellow member of the New Orleans Country Club, Janie Charbonnet, remembers meeting him in the Men's Grill on family day and noticing that he was wearing sunglasses indoors. "I thought perhaps he had just come in from playing golf and had forgotten to take them off," Janie reported. "I had no idea from the way he carried himself that he was blind. After all, he and his friends had obviously been playing golf, so how could he have been blind?"

Sherry had never imagined dating a blind man, and was still unaware that he was sightless when she met him for the first time. This occurred when she mentioned to her neighbors, Sally and Walter Baldwin that she wished to meet someone in New Orleans.

"Sally told me about a very fine gentleman she knew who lived in a nearby Uptown apartment with his friend Donny Doyle," Sherry said, "and asked if she could let him know about me. I agreed and she gave Pat my name and address which of course he couldn't read, so I didn't hear from him at first. It took him six months to find out who I was and get up the courage to ask me out.

"When he finally got around to it, I met him at his door and quickly realized that he was blind. I escorted him to the home of our neighbors and mutual friends, Pam and Grady Harper, for our blind date. Also there were Ben and Ruth Goliwas and Sally and Devereux Moring, all good friends whose company Pat obviously enjoyed." Everyone had a wonderful time dancing to an Andy Williams record and laughing all night at the witty antics of Grady and Pat.

"For me though," Sherry continued, "it was truly a case of the blind leading the blind because I was very inexperienced with dating, and Pat was, well, blind.

"One odd thing I remember about that evening is the painting of Pam and Grady in their home by Ruth Goliwas, a very fine artist. Pam had been a beauty queen at Tulane, and when I saw it I thought, *I hope if I get married someday, my husband and I will have a lovely portrait like that of ourselves in our living room.* And, of course, I eventually did, with Pat. But not until six years later!

"The artist who painted us, Verner Arber, once told me that most people think the soul of a subject is best seen in the eyes, but she believed that people revealed themselves more with their mouths than with their eyes. Perhaps that's true, because Pat had a lovely smile, and I never saw his eyes because he never took those dark glasses off on our dates. But that never stopped him from shielding his eyes with a hand whenever I was driving him and came to a quick stop. I suppose you never entirely get over a terrible trauma like that, but from what I could see, he was, nevertheless, a very well-adjusted gentleman, despite all he had been through.

"A friend called me the next day and asked my impression of my date with Pat. I told her he had a very nice voice. Shortly after that he phoned me and made some small talk, then said, "I was just wondering, um, if you would like to go out." I told him I would love to and we went to dinner with two other couples on a Saturday night. The next day I told a friend that I had had more fun with Pat that night than I had enjoyed in months.

"The next day he called me and told me his father was in Ochsner Hospital and asked if I would go with him to visit his dad, meaning of course that I would take him to see his father. I noticed that Pat's father was very kind and respectful when speaking to his wife, Pat's mother.

"I also remember Pat telling me that day how much he wanted to win an important golf game for his father. This was the blind golf national championship, of course, that had eluded him for several years. His father, Pat Sr., had been a marvelous athlete himself, and had recently been inducted into the Spring Hill Sports Hall of Fame, where he had played golf and football in college.

"The day after that visit Pat phoned me and said he had to go to a deposition out of town. He said it might take a few days but that he would be in touch afterwards. When he returned rather late one day, he asked if I would like to go to dinner. I had already eaten, but he said he had reservations for two at the Red Room on St. Charles Avenue, closed now but then a great live jazz venue. So I went with him, which is of course to say I drove us there. I was quite full and nervously pushed my pompano and crab meat around on my plate, nervous that he would think I wasn't enjoying myself. But nothing could have been further from the truth. Although I was ready to meet someone special, I was a little shy and largely untested on dates. But he was such a charming gentleman that he always immediately put me at ease."

Once again Sherry and Pat got along marvelously that evening and for many days afterwards, but Pat simply wasn't able to consider making a commitment of any kind to Sherry, despite how close to her he felt. There was the divorce, of course, that still bothered him, and Sherry was eleven years younger. Although he had reestablished himself with his law firm and was making an important contact with the Hibernia bank by handling more and more of their business, he still had a long struggle ahead reviving his golf game and preparing to take on world class competition.

Even so, their son, Patrick III, who didn't come along until 1981, nevertheless remembers how his parents related to each other from an early age. "It was quite ironic," Patrick said, "my mother was and is absolutely gorgeous, but dad never saw her. No one could say he married her for her looks. What he saw in her was her spirit, a fine person, just as selfless as he was. For her part, she loved him the same way, and never seemed to notice that he was blind since he never acted like he was handicapped."

However, there was no talk of marriage and sons in 1972. For the time being, Pat would settle for enjoying pleasant evenings with Sherry, for whom he felt great respect and affection. Yet his primary focus at that time had to be on excelling at blind golf and making it something other than the old cliché that the sport was "a good walk spoiled."

Or put another way, the lawyer and future bank president had to get a firmer handle on the game so he could play with top flight competition. Perhaps the all-time champion home run slugger, Hank Aaron, put it best– "It took me seventeen years to get three thousand hits in baseball. It took one afternoon on the golf course."

Pat had more than simply playing well in mind. He had wanted to win the USBGA Championship since he had read Charley Boswell's book, *Now I See,* several years earlier. But in 1972 he had an even more pressing motivation to win it; to win one for his father who was now ill with bladder cancer.

Pat's dad had been a great athlete himself, playing football, baseball and running track in 1925-26 at Spring Hill College in Mobile. Not only had Spring Hill inducted him into its athletic Hall of Fame, the college had awarded Pat Sr. the Porter Cup award for being the greatest athlete in a combination of athletic endeavors.

Like his son, Pat Sr. graduated from Tulane Law School and successfully practiced law in New Orleans. He had reared his son to be a good Catholic, an outstanding student, and a splendid multi-sport athlete, always supporting Pat in every sport his boy undertook.

But now Pat Sr. was fighting cancer, and knowing that his dad was quite ill and could very well pass before year's end, Pat urgently desired to win the 1972 USBGA championship. The tournament would be played once more in Greensboro, North Carolina, at the Starmount Forest Country Club, home of the hills that had bedeviled him in 1970.

Although Pat played well and led the tournament early on that August day, he faded at the end and lost once more. This time, though, the winner was not named Boswell or Lazaro.

Jim Daniel of Summerville, Georgia won his first and only blind golf national championship, scoring a two-day total of 187 while Charley Boswell shot a 200 to finish second. Pat shot a 207 to finish third, while his nemesis Joe Lazaro scored a final 209 strokes to finish fourth. Pat had fared decently the first day shooting a 99, but fired a 108 on Sunday, respectable but not good enough to prevail.

Sherry remembered that he claimed to have made a "silly mistake" on the last hole, securing a third-place finish. "He was really upset," Sherry said. "He really wanted to win that one for his dad, knowing he wouldn't live long enough to see Pat play another championship tournament. He really took that loss hard. It was as tough a loss as I ever saw him take."

As usual, Pat took the loss all on himself, assuring his coach Henry Sarpy that only his own errant shots had cost them the championship. His father and friends consoled him, as always with the same ironic witticisms he frequently offered them.

Tragically however, Pat's dad died of cancer two months later in October of 1972.

Pat eventually realized that his urgent need to press himself to win for his dad in Greensboro had played a major role in his eventual defeat. He resolved to gain better control of his emotions in the future. But in 1972, he had no choice but to accept the bitterest of defeats in his sporting career. Far worse, with the passing of his father, mentor and idol, and his failure to give his father a parting gift of a national championship, he had endured the most terrible loss he had suffered since his blindness-causing injury in 1966, and his divorce and separation from his beloved girls the next year.

Yet Pat Brown Jr., in large part due to the love and support his parents, friends and more recently, Sherry, had given him, and his deep and abiding faith in God and his own talents, was not going to let this or anything else defeat him, or stop him from reaching all his goals in golf or life.

5

WITHIN A WHISKER OF SUCCESS

They say love will find a way. I know determination will.
— Ronnie Milsap

Golf: A plague invented by the Calvinist Scots as a punishment for man's sins.
— James Barrett Reston

Pat and Sherry continued to date in 1973, their relationship growing at the same pace as Pat's improving golf game. But as Sherry recalls, Pat was having trouble making a commitment at that time. Memories of a failed marriage, the fear of loss of control over his own fate, and the problems another marriage might present to his daughters in Tampa were matters that Sherry felt were holding him back from taking the plunge a second time.

Sherry knew Pat was the right man for her. Always a gentleman, Pat was also a very strong person, a devoted Catholic, and a man for whom sightlessness, loneliness, the loss of loved ones, separation from his children, and the stress of practicing law without his sight could not overcome him or even slow him down.

She also felt she would be the right woman for him, if only she could make him see it. In time, she would devise a strategy that would force him to make a choice, but that was now several years in the future.

In the meantime, Pat was working on a plan to ensure

success in the USBGA National Championship of 1973. He and Henry Sarpy were assiduously working on conquering his greatest flaw at the time—inconsistency. They played regularly on various New Orleans courses and a few in Mobile, where Pat had owned a condo for years. Most of their practice and play came at Pat's home course, the New Orleans Country Club, where he had begun shooting consistently in the mid to high 80's. In fact he had improved to the point where he beat sighted golfers on that course far more often than not. His handicap was lowering, and he felt he and Henry were improving. But beating weekend golfers on a flat local course was hardly the same as defeating a Boswell or Lazaro on a hilly course in a faraway city before a crowd of six thousand spectators, with reporters reporting his every move back to the *Times-Picayune* for his friends and family to read.

In April 1973 the *Times-Picayune* reported that the New Orleans Country Club would host the USBGA National Championship Tournament in May. Tickets to the 36-hole match would cost $5, and a Pro-Am Celebrity Tournament would accompany the championship that would include Saints players Archie Manning, Dan Abramowicz, and Dick Gordon, as well as former basketball great Bob Petit and character actor and comedian Frank Gorshin, then famous for playing the Riddler on the popular *Batman* television show.

Later in May, professional golfer Fred Haas of New Orleans publicly challenged Pat and Charley Boswell to a four-hole match at the New Orleans Country Club on May 22nd—three days before the championship event would take place. Hass had won a national golf championship at LSU and five PGA tournaments in his career, and Self had captained the Clemson University golf team for two years. The challengers accepted two terms — they would play blindfolded and retain the blindfolds from the locker room to the final shot on the course.

Five days before the championship, Pat was in good spirits and feeling optimistic about winning both the challenge and the main event. He was especially happy with the support Henry Sarpy was giving him. Pat told the press that although Henry had only been married for a year and was practically a newlywed, he was working almost daily with Pat to help ensure a victory that year. As Pat told Ed Tunstall of the *Times-Picayune*, "Henry lines up every shot, gives me the distances, and selects a club. All I have to do is hit it."

One day Charley Boswell and Pat were getting in some licks on the practice tee at the club. The former, watching Pat hit, quipped, "I wish you wouldn't hit it so damned hard." With such compliments from his blind golf idol, Pat had every reason to be optimistic. So did Henry Sarpy, who noted at the time that Pat's consistency was improving substantially. "He just needs to keep up a good tempo," Henry often noted, "and make a smooth stroke without over swing." Something was working right, because Pat's smoothest strokes with his driver often garnered him a 230-plus-yard drive.

As much as he wanted to win a championship for himself, his coach and his hometown audience, Pat had another motivation that was far more important to him than winning. This was one that he had acquired from reading about and talking to his fellow blind golfers Charley Boswell and Joe Lazaro.

As Pat told Nancy Wesson with the *Times-Picayune,* "When the public sees blind golfers play in big tournaments, they get a different perspective. They see we're not just cup shakers." Hopefully, some other handicapped people will see that you don't have to sit in a rocking chair." By pointing this out to the world, Pat declared to Ed Tunstall of the *Times-Picayune,* blind golfers can "get the picture away from who's shaking the cup to the people who can do the job and live within certain limitations, and do their part in society and not be a burden on society."

Speaking to Tunstall a few days before the championship tournament, Pat allowed how it gave him a chance to do what he loved, mainly compete at golf, but also give the public a "chance to see what a non-sighted person can do." This he said, could possibly lead to employment for non-sighted people.

Pat went on to say how fortunate he always felt about his sight-robbing accident. Fortunate for being alive, first of all, but also for being a lawyer, handling the same kind of cases he had before the accident. "I try cases in court," he declared, "several days a week. Unlike a cab driver or a doctor, I had no problem."

He then waxed eloquent about his friends and competitors Charley Boswell and Joe Lazaro. "Charley's just fantastic," he urged, noting that Boswell had never played golf before losing his sight, while he [Pat] had enjoyed a handicap of between 2 and 7, and won a city championship of golf in college. He lauded Joe Lazaro for being a radar tube technician, i.e., a radar engineer, saying that Charley and Joe were "really something special."

In many of his interviews, Pat would explain how

blind golf was different, pointing out the grounding club rules in traps, and explaining that qualification for championship play involved scoring 120 or less several times and producing a doctor's note that one was sightless. This second requirement came about, he loved to report, after a golfer who had won the championship was walking off the course and sidestepping puddles, resulting in his disqualification and implementing the aforesaid requirement.

Two days later, on May 22nd, *Times-Picayune* sports writer Dave Lagarde reported that one Buster Williams would be driving the cart for Pat and Henry during the championship rounds, often making suggestions on club selection. Noting that Buster had earlier lost one foot, Lagarde explained that when the tall, lanky Pat was walking with his arm on the short and stocky Henry Sarpy's shoulder, and Buster was limping along beside them, they "looked more like a drum and fife corps then the 'onesome' they actually were." By onesome, Lagarde, a capable golfer himself, was repeating Pat's comment that he was not achieving his goals by himself; he was involved in a team.

A day later, on the 23rd, the blind challenge came about at the par 71, 6,481 yard-long New Orleans Country Club course, pitting pro golfers Fred Haas and Jimmy Self against Pat and Charley Boswell. According to *Times-Picayune* reporter Dave Legarde (who had also signed up for the forthcoming Pro-Am celebrity tournament two days later), it was truly a case of the "blind leading the blind," with the non-sighted golfers soundly whipping the blindfolded sighted ones. Although the Haas/Self team's driving skills were respectable, their short games proved infinitely less so, leading to their losses on all four holes, on two of which Pat shot par. Hass began having dizzy spells by the third hole, requiring him to remove his blindfold between shots. Once, when Haas skulled another finesse shot, his coach, Joe Edwards, told him, with a wink the blindfolded Haas never saw, "you didn't watch the ball on that one."

On May 25th, during the first round of the championship tournament, Pat teed off remembering that he had fallen apart to the Jim Daniels and coach David Carlock team the year before at Pinehurst, North Carolina, on a hilly course. But on his relatively flat home course, he felt he held an advantage over his competition. In this belief he was partly correct; he shot a 94 on a course soaked from two straight days of rain, while Charley Boswell shot a 96. However, Joe Lazaro shot a 92 to take the first day's lead.

Wind gusts of thirty-five miles per hour wreaked havoc with the golfers the second day. The wheels came off for Jim Daniels on the fifteenth hole, but he refused to blame the wind for his failures. His coach, David Carlock, did note that the cracked ribs Daniels was suffering from did hamper his ability to stroke the ball consistently.

Lazaro also had his problems, scoring an eight on the 12th hole and a nine on hole four. Boswell opened with a ten on the first hole, recovered for several holes, and then made an eight, nine, and ten consecutively.

"I was trying to guide the ball into the wind," Boswell told Lagarde, "instead of hitting it." Boswell's coach, Grant Thomas, observed that with the wind howling so loudly, the golfers could not hear their club head as they were bringing it back to swing at the ball.

Lagarde's headline on May 28th showed who won

the championship after the second day's round. It read "Lazaro's Dramatic Deuce Ends Blind Golf Event." Lazaro had sunk a three-foot putt on the third playoff hole with Boswell to end their match and claim the major title. Boswell, who hadn't gone down easily, had sunk a twenty-foot putt to halve the first playoff hole. Pat had three-putted the last hole from twenty-two feet to miss the playoff. Lazaro and Boswell had both shot 199, while Pat had finished the 36-hole tourney with a score of 200. Daniels had scored 204 to ensure that he did not repeat as champion.

In 1974 Pat was elected President of the USBGA and served in that capacity through 1992. The on-the-course golf news was not so happy, however, as Pat's championship blues continued that year. In the USBGA Championship tournament he finished second to the seemingly indomitable Joe Lazaro in Concord, Massachusetts at the Nashawtuc Country Club.

Although the losses in 1973 and 1974 were painful, especially with the collapse on the final hole in 1973, they paled by comparison to the 1972 loss when Pat failed to give his dad a championship win.

Yet all of them served as motivation for him to get over the hurdle and finally win the big one. The next chance would come in July of the next year, 1975, during the 33rd National Championship Tournament at the Belmont Country Club in Toledo, Ohio. That course was renowned for its fast, spacious undulating greens, and fairways lined with trees, six of which were guarded by "heart-stopping" water hazards.

Worse, Joe Lazaro and Charley Boswell would be there, waiting to hand him another heart-wrenching loss. On

June 10, 1975, Pat left for Toledo with Henry Sarpy in tow, his disappointing close losses in the previous two years weighing heavily on his mind. But Sarpy told Dave Legarde that "Pat's reaching a point of consistency that he has never had before. As you know," Henry concluded, "consistency has always been our biggest hurdle."

The question that remained for Pat, his family and friends, and his burgeoning New Orleans fan base, would that new consistency be enough?

6

A NATIONAL CHAMPION AT LAST

You must play boldly to win. The most rewarding things in life are often the ones that look like they cannot be done.

— Arnold Palmer

Light is the task where many share the toil.

— Homer

In 1975, the world would prove quite altered from what it had been in the optimistic post-war 1950s and 1960s. Communists would take over South Vietnam and the Vietnam War would come to an inglorious end. Gerald Ford, an avid golfer, who had succeeded the Watergate-plagued Richard Nixon as American president, would pardon Nixon, and as is often forgotten, also pardon Robert E. Lee. Charles Manson follower Lynette Fromme would attempt to assassinate Ford in September. Ronald Reagan, a former actor and Democrat turned Republican would announce that he would challenge Ford for the Republican nomination for presidential candidate, but not before New York City would be approved for a $6.9 billion dollar bailout.

The Cold War, the Space Race, energy crisis and Detente remained ongoing. Future Ole Miss coach Lane Kiffin would be born that year, along with actress Angelina Jolie and golfer Tiger Woods. Actress Susan Hayward and Black Muslim leader Elijah Muhammad would pass from the scene. Fire would break out in the World Trade Center, Bob Hope would host the Oscars and Muhammad Ali would destroy Joe Frazier in the Thrilla in Manila. *Saturday Night Live* would launch on NBC and *The Godfather II* would garner the Best Picture Oscar. The Reds would beat the Red Sox in the World Series despite Carlton Fisk's game-six heroics, and the Steelers would edge the Vikings in Super Bowl IX played in Tulane Stadium in New Orleans.

Also in Louisiana, Governor Edwin Edwards would bring his unique blend of wit and corruption to the Governor's mansion for a second term, where he would later say about a future race that, "I could not lose unless I was caught in bed with a dead girl or a live boy." Moon Landrieu would graduate from City Councilman to Mayor of New Orleans, where the Sugar Bowl would be played for the first time, won by Alabama. The Tulane Green Wave would post a 4-7 football record, ending a miserable season with an even more miserable 42-6 trouncing by a 4-7 LSU team that had already lost to rivals Ole Miss, Alabama, Texas A&M, and Florida by a combined score of 184-54.

But all would not be lost in 1975 for sports fans in Louisiana. An incredible athlete would continue striving for a championship, rising from a deep chasm of loss like the legendary phoenix that had risen from the ashes in ancient times. And this New Orleanian phoenix, like the mythical bird that died in a culmination of flames, had seen his championship hopes terminated in flaming collapses for the past few years. This, of course, was a former Tulane two-sport superstar named Patrick W. Browne Jr.

Born on April 14, 1933, in New Orleans, Pat had always

been a natural athlete as well as a top student and honor graduate of Tulane Law School. But it was as a star athlete that he gained the most recognition.

He had been selected to the American Legion All Star team after sporting a league-leading .484 batting average at Jesuit High School, where he also lettered in basketball and golf. At Tulane University he had joined the basketball team as a walk-on and became a three-year letterman and senior captain of the team, setting the single-game scoring record that stood for many years. He also captained the golf team.

At Tulane he also found time to win a City Junior Championship golf tournament and join the Delta Kappa Epsilon fraternity where he acquired a great love of enjoying the good life with his friends. After graduation he would soon acquire a reputation as the truest of southern gentlemen, a devout Christian without a hint of religiosity, a loyal friend, a devoted son and father, a successful attorney with Jones Walker, and last but not least, a near scratch golfer.

But both his athletic success and his marriage had come to a crashing halt when at the age of thirty-two he suffered an automobile accident that had deprived him of sight and subjected him to years of physical and emotional anguish.

Yet, he had come back from all that, resumed his legal career, spent a great deal of time with his daughters in Tampa, and made a life of sorts for himself with the help of his parents and close friends. He had even taken up golf again thanks to the urgings and support of his attentive companions, young and old.

But two key goals had as yet eluded him. Forging another family with a new wife and children, and framing a championship blind golf career around the USBGA and other national and international tournaments remained only a goal, not a reality. He was making some headway with the former goal, but he strove for the past six years alongside his steadfast coaches to achieve the latter aim, as yet with no success.

An opportunity to redeem himself on a seventh try finally came in 1975 when he and Henry Sarpy took on the world's premier blind golfers in Toledo, Ohio, for their next shot at the USBGA National Championship Invitational. The forty-two-year-old had recently been shooting in the 80s at the New Orleans Country Club, but that was his home course, and this would be the unfamiliar Belmont Country Club, fifteen hours and a thousand miles away. There, he would find his good friend and nemesis Joe Lazaro waiting.

Pat lost no time making his case for the championship on July 15th, shooting a 96 and taking a six-stroke lead over Jeff Jankot, from Brookline, Massachusetts, whose card showed a 102 first round score. Californian Charles Mayo was third at 104, with Jankot's fellow Massachusettsan, Joe Lazaro, in fourth place with a 107. Pat had aided his case by sinking a 20-foot birdie putt on the par-4 14th hole.

The next day in the second and final round, Pat, with the aid of coaches Henry Sarpy and Jay Weigel, the son of another law partner then matriculating at De La Salle High School, shot a 100 for a total score of 196 on 36 holes. Charles Mayo carded a 99 to finish with a second place total of 203, trailing Pat by a total of 7 strokes! Lazaro finished in fourth place scoring 210, while Boswell withdrew after the 14th hole, having posted a score of 110 the day before. The *Times-Picayune* headline that day read, "Pat Browne Captures Blind Golf Title."

"We finally did it!" Pat exclaimed. "It's been on my mind for six years, and we won it." Pat made a point of noting that he had not prevailed on his own. "We finally got over the hump! I feel total elation," he continued, "and I give thanks to God for letting us achieve this goal.

"This is the beginning," Pat declared. "We not only have the satisfaction of winning the tournament, but this lets people see that people without sight can live normal lives with the exception of not being able to see. That's what it's all about."

"Pat was very excited to finally win that championship," Sherry said with great understatement. "He had been so discouraged for losing to Charley and Joe before, and not winning for his father. After he won in 1975, he knew he could do it again, and boy did he ever!" Pat became so confident, Sherry continued, "that he began taking piano lessons. Monty Bee, Pat's friend and a Mississippi lawyer, declared that he would teach Pat how to play, and he did. Pat played with one hand and could pick out any song's melody."

This was the beginning of the very good times for Pat, who often went out on the town with his friend, and famous Commander's Palace restaurateur, Dick Brennan Sr., with whom he competed in high school basketball and then played with as teammates at Tulane. Both of them looked similar, tall and very Irish, were very witty, and knew how to live the good life. Gerry Barousse would later note the way the good friends would mess around with each other. Pat would often kid Dickie about how his restaurant bathrooms were dirty and the kitchens even dirtier, Barousse recalled. Then once when

Dickie was in Pat's apartment he crammed his foot in the bathroom trash can to make a point, only to get his foot stuck. Pat simply smiled and said, "I can't help you."

That good time included experiencing Mardi Gras in New Orleans. The Knights of Momus, the second oldest Mardi Gras society in New Orleans, chose Pat as King of its krewe, and he posed for a photo as king using his scepter as a golf club.

Pat as King of Momus, Mardi Gras Krewe, New Orleans, 2007, swinging his scepter like a golf club

Sarasota golf coach and longtime blind golf supporter Joe McCourt, befriended Pat at blind golf tournaments and discovered the many facets of Pat Browne Jr. "He was a very religious man," Joe said, "having been brought up that way, and he had a lot of confidence for a blind person. How many blind people do you know who will be walking along then suddenly start singing a song and doing a little of the old soft shoe dancing? Pat not only did that every now and then on the course, but he told me once that he played in a Pro-Am Tournament out west with Ray Bolger as his partner."

Ray Bolger was a famous Broadway singer and dancer in the 1930's and played the Scarecrow in the Wizard of Oz. "I asked Pat if he did a soft shoe routine with Bolger," Joe continued, "and he said, 'you better believe I did!"

But all the success and enjoyment aside, nothing ever changed Pat Brown's wonderful personality. "Winning never changed Pat in any way," Sherry offered. "He continued to give other people all the credit for his success, and took full blame for any failures on and off the golf course. And he was the same person as a champion as he was in high school when labored in the banana docks in New Orleans.

"Another thing about Pat that never changed," Sherry continued, "was his deep religious faith. Like his parents before him, he had attended Holy Name Catholic Church every Sunday, and he continued to do so just as religiously after winning championships. He never stopped attending week-long Catholic retreats near New Orleans every year. He believed that God had blessed him in rewarding his faith that he would eventually succeed in golf, love and life, and he never quit believing. When he was on the road he would always ask his coach to find the Catholic church nearest to where they would be playing, and attended there every weekend. And when he was in town, he had a friend drive him to mass every day of the week."

Former New Orleans insurance salesman and fellow New Orleans Country Club low handicap golfer Dick Meyers said that Pat continued to be an unbelievable, loving caring person, a man of great stature yet still so open and friendly with everyone. And they loved him for it.

"I saw him the first time in the 1970s," Dick said after he won it all in 1975, when he was playing in a Pro-Am tournament. At the time he was approaching a tee box after playing the 6th hole at Lakewood Country Club. The guy playing with me said, 'here comes the blind guy.' Pat proceeded to stroke a 250 yard drive, and this was in the days when we used a balata ball and wooden clubs. I thought that was impressive, but not as spectacular as how friendly he was to everyone in the clubhouse — other players, the club staff, the waiters, and the caddies even after he became the champ.

"He never lost his sense of humor, either," Meyers added. "Around that time he invited some people to his apartment for after work drinks. They found him fixing drinks in the dark, only to discover that he had removed all the bulbs from his lights! Pat simply never let anything get him down," Meyers concluded. "He never showed any resentment or blame about his accident or anything else. I tell you, Pat Browne Jr. was as fine a man as you could ever hope to know."

Archie Manning recalled that Pat was nothing if not just

"a regular guy." You would walk in the [New Orleans] men's club room, and you'd see him playing the piano and singing, having a glass of whiskey with his friends. Everyone loved Pat at the club. He was down-to-earth and the kind of guy who was friends with everyone he met."

But despite the elation he and his companions felt over winning the 1975 USBGA National Championship, they realized that the rest of Pat's career was not going to be a cakewalk. He still had challenges to face in the championship tournaments, practicing law, and finally having a second wife and hopefully, a son to go with his three lovely daughters.

How Pat would meet these challenges would eventually determine his legacy on and off the golf links. But it was in golf that he would publically establish himself as a perennial champion or a flash in the pan that faded at the first sign of pending defeat.

7

ON THE CUSP OF ULTIMATE SUCCESS

The more I practice, the luckier I get.

—Gary Player

Just because a man lacks the use of his eyes doesn't mean he lacks vision. I never thought of being blind as a disadvantage; blind doesn't mean you can't listen.

—Stevie Wonder

In November 1975, Pat reunited with Fred Haas, Lionel Herbert, and Bob Petit in a Cystic Fibrosis Pro-Am Celebrity tournament in New Orleans. Raising money for charity was part and parcel of what made Pat Browne Jr. the person he was. It surprised no one when he accepted another chance to remember others who had known suffering and loss.

The fires of competition also still burned as brightly in his soul as they ever had, and he gladly accepted the challenge to defend his blind golf championship title in 1976 at Hillwood Country Club in Nashville, Tennessee. His main competition there would be Jeff Jankot, the Bostonian he had soundly defeated in 1975.

The Hillwood course proved extremely difficult for Pat, with its rolling hills, long tree-lined fairways, and wickedly placed bunkers and water hazards. Typical of its challenges, the course's par-4 416 yard ninth hole offered an uphill tee shot to a dogleg right fairway.

Ultimately, the challenge proved too much for Pat, with a red hot Jankot and his coach Bob Bernier carding a total score of 188, a six-stroke margin over Pat and Henry Sarpy's 194. With a comment typical of those shared by such good friends, Dickie Brennan Sr. took Pat's arm and said, "Come on, ex-champ, let's get you a drink."

The next year Henry Sarpy retired as Pat's tournament coach and Gerry Barousse took over that position. He and Pat traveled to Akron, Ohio to play in the national championship at Firestone Country Club. One of golf's greatest courses, Firestone is consistently ranked among the Best Golf Courses in America and in the world by Golf Magazine and Golf and Travel Magazine. It features three courses, the North, South and Fazio courses, where, in 1975, Jack Nicklaus miraculously parred the South course's Arnold Palmer-named "Monster" 16th hole on his way to his fourth of five PGA Championships.

But such glory was not to crown Pat's head in September of 1977, as Nashvillian, Dave Meador, and teenage coach Stuart Smith prevailed. After gaining their victory in a sudden death playoff, Smith took Meador by the arm and sprinted him down the fairway in celebration. Pat, who was part of that playoff, finished third with a score of 104. On the first playoff hole he stroked a great tee shot, then hit a nine iron for a 110-yard shot to the pin, but his ball struck the top of a bunker. He took two shots to get out of the sand, causing him to lose the hole by a stroke. Meador had come from behind to tie Pat and force the playoff, which he won with an unbelievable sand shot and a ten-foot putt.

Meador had also lost his vision in a 1966 car wreck, but had overcome that as well as recurring cancer to become a successful insurance salesman, motivational speaker, author of the book, *Broken Eyes, Unbroken Spirit*, and a three-time champion of blind golf.

After his father had pushed him to take up blind golf, Meador soon realized that this was his chance to make a difference in life. "It [blind golfing] is a form of seeing more beautifully, richer and deeper than actual sight," he once said. "It's smelling the trees, hearing the birds in the distance; it's a restoration of sight."

He also rang a familiar tune among champion blind golfers when he said, "Golf is about what's possible for each of us," referring to both blind and sighted golfers. "When we forget that, we might as well be four dudes having breakfast together."

From 1967 to 1976, Pat and Henry Sarpy had beaten the best and lost to the best, and had enjoyed a wonderful friendship along the way. But Henry was in his forties by 1977, relatively newly married and looking to fully refocus himself in making a family and practicing law. It had been time for him to move on, retire from the hunt for national championships and look back fondly on his and Pat's drive to become the kings of blind golf. He would help out on a few days when Pat's new coach was unavailable, but 1976 spelled the end of his term as Pat's primary tournament coach.

Tragically, Henry Sarpy would be killed by a hit-and-run driver as he was leaving a wedding in 2016. But in 1976, he had the satisfaction of knowing that due to his great sacrifice of time and energy, he had guided a blind and shattered man from the depths of despair to the heights of glory as a national champion blind golfer, and earned the love and respect of all who knew him.

Thanks in part to Henry's efforts, the time for a new era in blind golf was fast approaching, and with the coming of Pat's new coach, Gerry Barousse in 1977, despite the initial lost championship that year, the world was about to discover something it had never even imagined before.

Baseball had known Babe Ruth, boxing had crowned Muhammad Ali, and professional golf was experiencing the emergence of Jack Nicklaus, all of whom would stand as the greatest of all time in their professions. All three of them would become more than just athletes. They would remember those less fortunate than themselves and in turn be remembered for their humanity as well as their athletic talents.

Yet they had accomplished everything with the benefit of sight and by starting to hone their talents in the springtime of their lives. In 1978, a middle-aged blind man, with the help of another very accomplished man half his age, was about to take the world of blind golf to a previously unimagined level. And he would do it all the while remembering those who had suffered as he had, and doing all he could to afford them an opportunity to accomplish all they desired despite their permanently darkened path.

8

A DYNASTY BEGINS

Love may be blind, but if you've ever known a blind person,
they still know where everything is.
— Opera singer Robert Breault

What a blind person needs is not a teacher, but another self.
— Helen Keller

Gerard Barousse Jr., Gerry to his friends, was born in New Orleans, where he attended Country Day School and became the Louisiana State Junior Golf Champion. He achieved the status of All-American golfer at Washington and Lee University. Yet he would never have guessed that he would become the best blind golf coach of all time while becoming a successful New Orleans businessman and real estate developer. He would marry and have three wonderful children, and put back into his community as an innovative benefactor.

In 1977 he replaced Henry Sarpy as Pat's tournament coach but they lost to Dave Meador in a three-way play-off, not the best start anyone had wanted. After all, Pat had vanquished the very best to become blind golf's national champion, and Gerry had himself been a national champion in his youth. Best golfer and best coach should reap national championships, they figured, but as yet, they hadn't achieved it together anywhere except in their imaginations.

69

Nike's Just Do It print ad with Pat and Gerry Barousse, 1988

So they got to work.

Joe McCourt remembered that Pat was easy to coach because he was such a great golfer, and so was Gerry Barousse. "They understood each other perfectly and developed a consistency that I've never seen before in years of following blind golf," McCourt said.

The 1978 National Championship Tournament would be played at Prestwick Country Club in Canton, Ohio, so Pat and Gerry began working together in earnest early that year. With Gerry being young and unattached, and with his expertise in golf as a past youth champion and collegiate All-American, the two had the time and past experiences to quickly become a formidable team.

On the first day of the 36-hole tournament, Pat took an early lead over Joe Lazaro, carding a 93 to Joe's 100. He and Gerry achieved this despite their 8 on the 18th hole, and the disaster at number seven. On that par-5 tee box they had enjoyed a ten-stroke lead, until the water hazard came into play.

"I don't tell him about the hazards," Gerry said, "I just tell him how far to hit it. I tell him about the water in practice, and of course he remembers it, but why belabor the point? Anyhow, he hit it right in there. I found the ball at the water's edge, but he couldn't take a full swing there, so he punched it out low. We took a ten on that hole, but still had the lead after the first day."

The next day, Pat fired a 104 for a total of 197, while Joe Lazaro shot a 106 to finish third with a 206. Defending champion Dave Meador shot a 99 that Sunday to finish with a 203 total to take second place.

Pat and Gerry did it, and did it together.

According to Gerry, this win gave Pat the confidence to believe he could win the championship on a regular basis. However, some things about Pat had not changed at all. "He was in some ways a creature of habit," Gerry recalled. "He would return to the same hotel and restaurants that he enjoyed the time before, and attend the same church he did the last time we were in town."

Pat's sense of playfulness had not changed either, as Gerry became acutely aware. After winning in Canton, and a few celebratory drinks, Pat challenged Gerry to a chipping contest in their hotel room at midnight. One of Pat's errant shots broke a twelve-inch glass bowl.

Pat's fun was not limited to the continent of North America. He often traveled with his friends to play golf around the world, and once when in England, he and Pepe Colomes decided to have some good-natured fun at a rental car clerk's expense.

Previously, at a blind golf tournament in America raising money for charity, Pat had met an executive with Avis rental car, a company he had represented in Louisiana. They got along well and the executive told Pat he would send him an Avis VIP card, so Pat could rent a car for free.

Now in England, Pat wanted to use his VIP card to rent a car for him and his friends. That was when the fun began. They located an Avis rental office and Pat strolled up to the counter. He produced his card for a free rental and asked the clerk to honor it.

"Certainly, sir," she said, looking at Pat closely, "Have you had a good day so far?"

"Yes," Pat exclaimed with a grin, "I'm having a lovely day, my friends and I are from New Orleans and we're here playing golf and having a great time."

The clerk leaned over the counter to get a better look at Pat, who promptly turned his head to the side. "My buddies will be here in a minute," he said.

As if on cue, Pepe entered the office. Pat said, "Ah he's here. This lady," he said, attempting to point to her but pointing in the wrong direction, "has been waiting for you." Then he turned toward the clerk, but faced far to her right, and said, "We would like to rent two cars, please."

She cast a mystified glance at Pepe and said, "Is he blind?"

Pat, turning to address her, but again looking in the wrong direction, says nonchalantly, "Why yes I am."

Pepe then said," May we have two cars, please?"

The clerk recovered herself before saying, "I'm sorry but I cannot rent a car to a blind person."

"That's ok," Pepe replied. "Look, don't worry about it.

We have a rope that I hold out the window in the front car and he holds out the window in the second car. I pull once so he knows to stop. We do this all the time."

"We do have a little trouble over here," Pat admitted, "with driving on the wrong side of the road."

"Come on in boys," Pepe said, and their two other friends came in and the clerk breathed a healthy sigh of relief.

Pro golf champion Payne Stewart had once said that, "I don't think it's healthy to take yourself too seriously. A bad attitude is worse than a bad swing." The greatest champions such as Babe Ruth, Henry Aaron, Campy Campanella, Muhammad Ali and many others had never taken themselves too seriously with the consequence of sometimes being criticized for clowning. Yet their fun-loving attitudes kept them loose and helped them become world champions many times over. And their flamboyant personalities only made them more attractive to the opposite sex.

And so it was with Pat and Sherry.

"He always had a great sense of humor," Sherry said. "But there was a great deal more to him than that. He was also a very reliable, wonderful person. He had so much faith in God, believing that he would never be given more than he could handle. Pat was very romantic in a subtle way. Very loving, loved his daughters very much, and couldn't wait to have more."

There was one problem, though, that was no laughing matter.

"He was terrified of getting into a situation like he had before where he had no control over what was happening in his life," Sherry said. "His wife had bailed on him, he had said, and he had difficulty overcoming that. I was flabbergasted when he told me that. We had been dating six years and I began to feel that he would never be able to take the next step, even though I knew with all my heart that we were perfect for each other."

So Sherry left town and stopped seeing him for a month. When she returned, he asked her what her plans were for the summer. "I'm going to San Francisco for three months," I told him.

"When he asked why, I told him he was such a chicken, and with no reason whatsoever. He was ten years older than me, blind, divorced with three daughters and I was not scared about any of that. Six months later he proposed to me and we were married."

Sherry and Pat were wed in New Orleans on August 11, 1979 at St. Andrews Episcopal Church on Carrollton Avenue. Although the newlyweds were both Roman Catholic, Pat's annulment from his first marriage was taking longer than they cared to wait, so they opted for a wedding in an Anglican Catholic Church, the closest thing available.

"After that we were always together," Sherry said. "Always close. He was fond of telling his friends that he had out punted his coverage when he married me, meaning I was a better wife than he deserved. But that was far from the truth. I was very lucky to meet him on that blind date. I could never have found anyone like him. He was the most wonderful person in the world."

Pat retired from practicing law with Jones Walker in 1979, a move that usually gave husbands and wives more time together. But this was no typical retirement, as Pat simply changed professions to become president and

CEO of the Hibernia Homestead Association, later the Hibernia Bank. And he was still wed to the "first love" from his youth, the game of golf. But this love of sport and competition brought Sherry and Pat closer together rather than keeping them apart.

For where golf was concerned, Sherry had been very supportive and would be with him all the way, win, lose or draw. "He had been very discouraged after losing the championship so many times to Charley Boswell and Joe Lazaro," she said. "But after he finally beat them in 1975, he began to believe that he really could win. And after he and Gerry won in 1978, he never again doubted that he would win it every year."

"Oh, they worked very hard at it," she continued. "He and Gerry, practicing every day at the New Orleans Country Club. But he was always very positive. Of course he would be nervous during those tournaments, but as he said, 'Why would I be playing if it didn't make me at least a little nervous?'

"But at the same time he was very humble," Sherry concluded. "It was always 'we won,' never 'I won.' And he truly believed he and Gerry were a team — a team that couldn't be beaten. And after he finished golfing, he and I were a great team, too.

"And I really believe that God picked him for that and for me. He was the chosen one, the only one who could handle it all like he did. So I hung in there with him all the way. Sometimes it was a challenge, being responsible for him every minute of every day, but it was well worth it. I consider myself the lucky one."

Loving hindsight by a devoted wife can explain some things, but Pat and Gerry had only won two championships at the time, and it had taken Pat seven tries to finally win the first one. Was Pat going to become the Jack Nicklaus of blind golf, or the Gay Brewer of blind golf? Brewer, a fine pro golfer in his own right, nevertheless found that winning the 1967 Masters Tournament would be the highlight of his career. After that win he never finished better than sixth in a major PGA tournament and did not win a tour event for the next five years.

Pat was far from being recognized as the Jack Nicklaus of blind golf after 1978, no matter how hard he and Gerry worked. Nicklaus would go on to win eighteen major PGA tournaments. How many USBGA championships and other blind majors would Pat win?

That picture began coming into focus the next year in 1979.

In June of that year, Pat and Gerry traveled to Pittsburg, Ohio to compete in the 34th USBGA National Championship tournament at Fox Chapel Golf Club. This course was and is famous for its template holes, or holes following, but not copying, famous holes on other courses, often those in Scotland. Princeton-educated civil engineer Seth Raynor designed Fox Chapel, using templates from many different, difficult holes.

The greatest difficulty every golfer but one faced on this course was playing against Pat Browne Jr. and Gerry Barousse. They carded a 93 both days, finishing with a 186, *twenty-two strokes* ahead of second place finisher Charles Mayo, at 208.

Giddy with excitement for having won by such a margin, Pat and Gerry later put together an amazing round of 80 at Pinehurst #2 in North Carolina. The year 1979 had been a great year for Pat, but the next year would prove one of the greatest years of his golfing life.

In 1980, Pat shot rounds of 75, 74, 79 and 75 at Mission Hills Golf Club in Palm Springs, California, during a Dinah Shore Pro-Am. These scores constituted the lowest four consecutive rounds ever fired by a blind golfer, and the 74 was the lowest single round ever shot by one.

That hot hitting was about to help launch Pat into a golfing universe previously unknown to and uncharted by blind golfers worldwide.

Pat and Gerry would enter and win many international tournaments in their day, but traveling with their golfing buddies was the most enjoyable part. Gerry Barousse remembers a trip to Scotland with some of their friends to play the Old Course at St. Andrews.

"It was Pat and me," Gerry said, "with Pepe Colomes, Buddy Lane, Ken Sayer and all their wives. We played the course and Pat shot an 85. That evening, Buddy took all the women to the Royal Edinburgh Military Tattoo Festival, a musical performance by the British Armed Forces and international military band on the Esplanade of Edinburgh Castle, and the guys all went back to our hotel for dinner and drinks.

"We were staying on the fourth floor of the Rusacks Hotel, and our room overlooked the 18th green at St. Andrews," Gerry recalled. "Our room had a five-by-five-foot parapet outside our window with a gravel floor. We had had a few drinks, and Pepe and I decided to take Pat's wedge and chip onto the green. Pepe held my belt as I swung, and my shot landed four feet from the hole. I returned the favor and Pepe's shot landed ten feet from the hole. We took Pat's putter and went down to the green to try to make our putts.

"Pat, standing on the balcony in his underwear, told Pepe he would never make his ten-foot putt. Sure enough, he missed it. But with Pat and his friends, no one ever missed a good time."

Pat was now an undisputed champion and a force to be reckoned with on the links, and the odds-on favorite to remain USBGA national champion. But he would soon find even more goals to achieve in life, golf, and in service to humanity.

9

WINNING ONE FOR THE HOME FOLKS

Do good and good will come to you.

— Aman Mehndiratta

Golf is the infallible test. The man who can go into a patch of rough alone, with the knowledge that only God is watching him, and play his ball where it lies, is the man who will serve you faithfully and well.

—P. G. Wodehouse

The Bible says that if you seek to acquire faith, act as if you have it, and it will eventually come your way. It's hard to say in retrospect if anyone believed in early 1980 that Pat Browne Jr. would become the greatest blind golfer of all time, but there was no doubt that he was beginning to believe it. If he was still plagued with any nagging doubts, those would dissipate like fog on a scorching sunny day as the year unfolded.

It certainly brought an auspicious beginning when, in February at the New Orleans Rotary Club, the USBGA presented Pat with his 1979 Champion's Jacket. In May, *Times-Picayune* sports editor Bob Roesler announced that the USBGA National Championship would be played at the New Orleans Country Club in June with famed professional golfer Byron Nelson as honorary chairman.

Pat was the favorite to win, but there were two other very talented entrants in the New Orleans tournament

With Byron Nelson, celebrity tournament partners at New Orleans Country Club

with very close ties to the favorite. Charley Boswell had retired from blind golf in 1976, but Pat had prevailed upon him to appear one last time in the Crescent City. George Riviere, a successful New Orleans businessman who had been blinded in an accident, would also qualify for play. Prior to the tournament, George reported to the *Times-Picayune* that as he laid in his hospital bed in complete darkness and despair, he received a phone call from USBGA president Pat Browne Jr. who told him that there were many worse things than being blind, and that he should never give up. Upon discovering that George was out of the hospital, Pat immediately took him to a course to practice sightless golf.

A year earlier in the 1979 championship, Riviere shot a

respectable 215 and received the USBGA's Most Improved Player trophy. He was now the dark horse favorite to upset Pat in future national championship tournaments.

On June 17 sports editor Dave Lagarde of the *Times-Picayune* reported that Pat was uncharacteristically declaring that he had become a "much more consistent golfer," and predicting that he and Gerry Barousse had a legitimate chance to "shoot some awful low numbers." This had recently been the case, as they had shot 84, 80, 86, 88 and 87 in their last five rounds on the 6,223-yard, par-71 New Orleans Country Club course.

Pat told Lagarde how many friends had noted that he was "uptight" when he played and lost the 1973 championship in New Orleans. "It hadn't been fear of playing before a crowd of people," he told Lagarde, as he had done that playing basketball at Tulane. Rather he was simply "scared to death" in general, which had given him a case of the "shanks" and led to an out-of-bounds shot and a 10 on the easy par-3 10th hole.

He was once more struggling in December of 1979 during pre-tournament practice rounds when one of his coaches, high school student Jimmy Self, helped him turn his game around.

Pepe Colomes added that he had observed that turn-around. "Pat," he recalled, "was playing like any other self-taught City Park player — all wrists. What's more, he was developing an outside arc swing. Jimmy helped him turn it around and now Pat was playing as good as he ever had." This was partly, Lagarde reported, because Jimmy had also helped Pat improve his short game by getting him to properly shift his weight, firming up his left wrist, and getting his legs involved in the swing.

At New Orleans Country Club

Several weeks before the USBGA Championship in New Orleans, Pat had been on the verge of breaking 80 in a round on his home course when he double-bogeyed the last two holes, missing his goal by one stroke. "I choked," he admitted, thinking about the score and not the proper swing. Such thinking had recently resulted in Pat's difficulties with hanging his club up in the grass on his backswing, then concentrating on that rather than making a proper full swing.

Lagarde reported that, for all his recent difficulties, Pat had not faltered in his daily practice routine of hitting balls on the practice tee at 4:30 a.m. and playing until 7:30 p.m. when it got dark with his coaches Gerry Barousse, Jay Weigel, and Jimmy Self.

Left to right: Pat's coaches, Patrick, Gerry Barousse, David Clarke, Charles Monsted, 2016, Sarasota, Florida

Would all that hard work pay off in the championship rounds, or would Pat again grow nervous before the home crowd? Would he focus on other than making a proper swing, and choke away this prime opportunity to show New Orleans blind golf fans that he had become America's premier blind golfer?

His friend George Riviere felt the odds favored Pat. On the eve of the championship he declared to the *Times-Picayune* that "Pat's in a league by himself."

"It's Pat then the rest of us, but he deserves it," George persisted. "We're about to spend two days chasing Pat."

For his part, Pat appeared very confident. "We've worked, we're prepared, we're ready," he told the press, sounding not unlike Caesar's famous "Came, saw, conquered," sans the arrogance.

Byron Nelson, winner of sixty-four PGA tournaments and five major championships, echoed that notion when he told *Times-Picayune* sports editor Peter Finney that he marveled at what Pat could do, and the touch he and other blind golfers had around the greens.

The Celebrity Pro-Am tournament matching blind and sighted golfers proved an entertaining companion to the hotly contested championship rounds. The team of Frank Lattiere, Dave Nelson, Dan Ryan and Allen Stern shot a 60, edging Pat, Byron Nelson, James Hanemann, Eric Hilton, and Sam Algood by a stroke. Lattiere's birdie-putt on the last hole, thanks to a tee shot eight feet from the pin, closed the deal. The team with Charley Boswell, Joe Lazaro, and Archie Manning surprised all by failing to make the winner's circle.

On June 28, the 35th USBGA Championship took place as planned at the New Orleans Country Club on a "windswept" day that caused bedlam with the golfers. Pat's wedge and putter tasked him all day, leading to a quadruple bogey on the second hole, and four three-putt greens. George Riviera suffered a similar fate, getting "stuck in double bogeys on the back nine." The end of the day tally, Dave Lagarde reported, found Pat with a first round 92, Riviere second at 95, and Dave Meador third with a 97. Joe Lazaro shot a 103 and Charles Mayo entered the clubhouse with a 105.

A bothered but still leading Pat Browne Jr. promised a "substantially better round" the next day. George Riviere, knowing he would be paired with Pat on Sunday, said, "I'm anxious to play with Pat tomorrow. I really believe I can shoot a 90 at him."

Appraised by his friend's comments, Pat smiled and said, "You tell George let's tee it up. I'm ready to go!"

That Pat was ready proved a great understatement. On Sunday's second and final round, he shot a blind golf championship world record 86, making his 178 the lowest blind golf championship round in history (besting Lazaro's 179). Riviere carded an impressive 92 to finish second with a 193. Meador was third with a 201.

The Sugar Bowl responded by bestowing its Sugar Bowl Athlete of the Month award upon Pat. More significantly, Pat could now take satisfaction that he was a three-time national championship winner, the most recent win coming on his home course. He now carried a 17 handicap on that course, where he frequently beat sighted golfers straight up without resorting to handicapping.

But the USBGA championship was not the only major he would win in 1980. The Guiding Eyes Classic had begun play in Mount Kisco, New York in 1978, inviting totally blind golfers to compete in what would become known as the "Masters" of blind golf. A "Corporate Scramble" the day after the tournament would pair blind golfers and benefactors to raise money for the training of guide-dogs for blind- and vision-impaired users, as well as for training the users to work with their dogs.

Ken Venturi, a pro golfer with 14 PGA tour wins and a victory in the 1964 U.S. Open, and a premier golf broadcaster and color commentator for CBS sports from 1967 to 2002, served as the Guiding Eyes' celebrity host. Clarence Campbell and his son and coach Warren Campbell had won the event in 1979, but for the next decade, a new champion would emerge. Pat and Gerry Barousse won the 1980 Classic and dominated this "Masters" championship just as they did the "Open," the USBGA Championship invitational tournament.

Meanwhile Pat and Sherry continued to enjoy New Orleans, their friends and their marriage in the early 1980s. In November of 1980 the New Orleans Country Club Board of Governors Ball feted Pat and Sherry, honoring him for winning the championship in New Orleans. During romantic dinners at the great New Orleans restaurants, they made plans for starting their own family. They had moved to what would become their permanent residence in Uptown New Orleans in 1975, and were ready to try for the son they both keenly hoped for.

On January 8, 1981, Sherry gave birth to Patrick W. Brown III at Ochsner Hospital, the very place where an ambulance had driven a broken Pat in 1966 to recover from the accident that had blinded him. Now, he and Sherry could enjoy the birth of a son, one who, apart from bringing them great familial joy, would one day play a major role in the extraordinary history that his now forty-seven-year-old father was making.

But eventually Pat's attention turned back to his teenaged "first love," the game of golf. In September 1981, he and Gerry Barousse traveled to Cleveland, Ohio, to participate in the USBGA National Championship at Acacia Country Club, There they won their fourth title, finishing three strokes ahead of George Riviere, 193 to 196. Dave Meador came in third with a 201 while Joe Lazaro finished a distant fourth. Pat had trailed Meador by three strokes the first day, but on the second day he overcame a 9 on the par-5 6th hole to make back-to-back pars on the next two holes to salt away the win.

Pat credited his driver and putter play for the improvement, "I kept it in play and got in the hole when I had to," he said. For his part, winning coach Gerry Barousse declared how thankful he was to have learned so much about patience from Pat. He was also very appreciative of how his teammate had taken him to the world's great courses, including St. Andrews, Pinehurst, Palm Springs' Winged Foot, and New Jersey's Baltusrol.

In October of 1982, on the Bryan Municipal Course in Greensboro, North Carolina, Pat and Gerry crushed all thirty national championship opponents en route to shooting 85 and 83 for a total of 168, besting the second place finisher by twenty-six strokes! On the back nine the second day Pat shot a 36, the first time that had been done in a blind golf tournament.

As Gerry Barousse related to the *Times-Picayune*, things may have gotten out of hand early in Greensboro. Pat bogeyed the last two holes on the front nine the first day.

On the way from the ninth green to the tenth hole tee box, Gerry took Pat aside and had a little chat. "I told him 'let's settle down and play our game.'"

Pat proceeded to par number ten and birdie eleven, and never looked back. "He only bogeyed the par-3 seventeenth because he hit a good shot that hit the top lip of a bunker. But during that time it was magical when he was hitting it so well."

That magic continued in 1983 when Pat and Gerry returned to the Acacia Country Club in Cleveland to win their sixth-straight national championship title. There they shot a 96 and 92 for a 188 total, seventeen strokes better than second place finisher Charles Mayo's 205.

The wizardry saw no drop-off at the 1983 Guiding Eyes Classic in Mount Kisco where Pat and Gerry had lost to Charles Mayo and his son Steven back in 1981. Pat began another unprecedented winning streak at the "Masters of blind golf," winning the 1982 tournament with Jimmy Self for the first of his fifteen consecutive titles through 1997. He won many of those with Gerry Barousse, but other coaches leading him to victory during the streak included David Clark (95, 97), Charles Monsted (85, 86) and Chris Shuler (83, 84).

Many good times followed for the Brownes—dining at Galatoire's, the Bon Ton Cafe and the Crescent City Steakhouse for relaxation between tournaments. Although, they spent every Sunday morning ensconced at a pew in Holy Name Catholic Church.

Or as Gerry put it, "He never stopped living the Jesuit (High School) way. Discipline, courage and faith were instilled in him at Jesuit and by his parents, and he never forgot it. Of course he was never going to quit, never stopped trying to prove himself to his daughters, to Sherry, and later to his son Pat. I suppose that's what drove him to the heights of success that he achieved.

"Sherry and Pat had a wonderful relationship," Gerry maintained. "He loved Sherry so much. He always said he outkicked his coverage with her, but one hundred percent of the time they both treated each other so well. Sherry wanted Pat to earn the right to lead. She always pushed him in all the right ways, leading in the community and loving all his children the right way."

"He was a southern gentleman by measures," she always said of Pat. "He was a graceful gentleman with a wonderful sense of humor."

Pat did indeed have a great sense of humor, although not all the humor was intentional. "Once Pat was walking back to his house from the clubhouse." Gerry said. "Sherry had closed the glass back door and he walked right through it. Sherry said he left a Pat-shaped hole in it."

Pat's wry sense of humor came out in various forms, including using his blindness to poke fun at others. "One time," Sherry said, "when we were out of town and staying in a hotel, a bus hit an electric pole and knocked out the lights in our room. In pitch black dark, I was struggling to get around without hurting myself. Pat laughed and said, 'you'd make a terrible blind person'."

Sherry recalled another conversation related to her by Preston Wailes, when he recalled the time had just finished working out at the country club when he overheard Pat talking to Sherry on the phone, needing a ride home from the club. Realizing from the conversation that Sherry would be unable to come get him anytime soon, Wailes offered to give Pat a ride to his Uptown home.

During the ride, Pat inquired as to whether Wailes considered him to be a good friend. When Wailes hesitated to answer what appeared to be a loaded question, Pat said, "Do you consider yourself to be a good friend? Because my good friends think it's funny to drop me off at the wrong house."

"I don't think we are good enough friends for me to do that to you," his companion replied.

Then there was the time before Pat and Sherry had met, when Pat had been enjoying a party with his good friends, realtors Ben Goliwas and Grady Harper, and their wives, Ruth and Pam, respectively. Pat approached Ben and said to the laughter of all in the party, "Your wife Ruth is really lovely, Ben. Do you mind if I braille her?"

"There's no doubt in my mind, Sherry said, "that Pat's sense of humor, especially having to do with his lack of sight, along with his faith in God and in himself, were what helped him overcome his difficulties after the car wreck. He never let anything keep him down, and that he could laugh at himself and others in a gentlemanly way was a big part of his handling his difficulties."

One of Pat's coaches, Gerry Barousse, also never lacked for a humorous view of life. "Once while playing in an international blind golf tournament in New Zealand, Pat became irritated waiting a long time for a second shot," Gerry related. "I decided to loosen him up by telling him that one of his competitors had his binoculars out again."

"What?" he groused. "That's illegal!"

"Needless to say," Gerry smiled, "we won that tournament like we did all of them in the 80s, in British Columbia, Australia or America."

Pat was now in a position to enjoy life as never before

after the accident, and nowhere more than in the men's locker room or Men's Grill at the New Orleans Country Club. Archie Manning recalled how Pat would play the piano and sing for the fellows there. "Everyone at the New Orleans Country Club loved Pat," Archie said. "They even named a tournament after him."

Men's locker room 'club' attendant, Lee Barlow, remembers that Pat enjoyed a glass of chardonnay with ice cubes, but whether drinking or not, he never lost his way in the clubhouse, and could navigate it so perfectly that if you didn't know him, you'd have thought he was wearing those sunglasses just for style."

"They were so fond of him there, that they had a painting made of him taking a swing and hung it on the wall," Lee added with a grin. "One of his friends told him that, for a joke, they had the artist portray the Tulane Green Wave grad and athlete dressed in LSU purple and gold colors. But don't you worry, they told him, you'll never see it."

But all the fun never kept Pat's mind off doing what he could to ameliorate the suffering many endured in life, the humility he retained while doing so. As he had once said at a scholarship presentation for a Brother Martin High School baseball pitcher who had overcome being born without fingers on one hand, "A handicap can be a blessing and mine certainly was. I see the benefit of being unable to see when I encourage other people who have lost their vision...That might sound like the other people benefit, and I hope they do. But the truth is that I do walk away as the beneficiary because there is no better reward than when you feel like you successfully helped another person."

Painting hanging in New Orleans Country Club

February of 1984 found him appearing at yet another charitable event, this time the Breakfast of Champions to raise money for leukemia patients. Also in attendance were LSU All-American roundballer "Pistol" Pete Maravich, Tulane head football coach Wally English, and New Orleans Saints players Lindsey Scott, Jeff Groth, Jim Pietrzak and Ken Bordelon.

Then it was back to work.

In June of 1984, Pat and coach Chris Schuler, a De La Salle High School student and fine golfer in his own right, participated in the Guiding Eyes Classic in Mount Kisco, New York, winning the "Masters" by carding a 101. As always, Pat helped raise thousands for the training of guide-dogs for the blind.

Pat had now won five of the first seven Guiding Eyes Classics that had been played. But that was not foremost on his mind. As usual, he spoke out for the handicapped, telling the *Times-Picayune,* "Basically our folks are employable and can be contributing members of society." He declared his belief that most handicapped people desired to work and contribute to society, and that earning a living "increased their self-esteem." And once again he gave credit to God for not giving him more than he could handle.

On a more humorous note, Chris Shuler noted that while in Mount Kisco on the practice tee, Pat hit a slice, then a hook, then a straight shot.

"What's it look like?" Pat asked.

"Another Easter Egg hunt," Chris deadpanned.

But the June 29, 1985 USBGA Championship proved no Easter egg hunt for Pat and Gerry, who won their ninth and eighth straight blind golf championship at the extremely challenging Riviera Country Club in Los Angeles. They shot 100 and 98 for a 198 total, beating second place finisher Charles Mayo by fifteen strokes. Their win broke Charley Boswell's string of seven straight championships. The highlight came when Pat made an incredible putt on a two tiered green, sending his ball toward the pin 76 yards away, around a devilishly placed trap, to within eight feet of the cup.

As always, Pat gave credit where he believed it was due. He told *Times-Picayune* staff writer Quin Hillyer that he credited Gerry Barousse for coaching him into the shot. Gerry told him that the putt was about 76 feet long, but the ball would "die just past a ridge 44 feet away," then break right and roll down a slope.

Pat went on to report that he felt that this was the toughest course they had ever played, long (over 7,000 yards) and with a 20-25 mile per hour wind blowing the entire tournament. But he wasn't finished passing out accolades to those he believed deserved them.

"Blind golf is a team game," he declared, "Success is due 60% to the coach." He then asserted that he had enjoyed "absolutely the best coaches," then saluted Gerry, Henry Sarpy, Chris Schuler, Jimmy Self and Charles Monsted.

Pat then said how excited he was to put on a future exhibition for the London Society for the Blind. He hoped to get blind golf going in England, he said, and have United States teams playing British teams, "Before I get too old."

Few doubted that, in 1985 Pat Brown Jr. was in any imminent danger of becoming too old to win blind golf championships on any continent. He was continuing to stroke the ball with authority, and enjoyed superlative health for a fifty-three-year-old. And the fires of competition were still burning white hot within him.

But he had another reason to remain young for many years to come. He was married to a wife ten years his junior, and they now had a four-year-old son. As many older dads know, nothing keeps a man younger than a growing son who insists upon it with every word and deed.

10

A Champ Gets His Due

Achievements on the golf course are not what matters; decency and honesty are what matter.

—Tiger Woods

As you walk down the fairway of life you must smell the roses, for you only get to play one round.

—Ben Hogan

February of 1986 found Pat Brown Jr., the chairman of Hibernia Homestead and Savings Association, explaining to the public via an interview with the *Times-Picayune*, that fixed loan rates were not always permanently fixed. Pat explained that they could be temporarily lowered based on various factors that he explained.

The newspaper had sought out Pat's guidance because he was as well-known in New Orleans for his business and banking acumen as he was for his legal expertise and golfing skills.

Bobby Crifasi, who would serve as comptroller, vice president and later general manager of the New Orleans Country Club, had many occasions to observe that acumen in action.

"I knew Pat while serving as president of the board of governors at the country club and found him easy to get to know. Of course he played golf often, but he did all the things other guys did, too. We went to an NBA game one time and he took his radio and stood and clapped like everyone else. I knew he rode in a Mardi Gras parade, went fishing occasionally, and enjoyed four-day Catholic retreats at Manresa, a Jesuit retreat center in Convent, Louisiana near New Orleans. But I was surprised to find how sharp he was with finances and numbers.

"I was a CPA and thought I had a good understanding of finances," Bobby recalled, "but Pat Browne was truly something else. At the first board meeting I had with him, he had his secretary read him all the board materials. He had a photographic memory, and once she read it to him, he had it down in his mind. In another board meeting, Pat said, 'Bobby, I notice the payroll is up,' citing a specific number, say $10,462, 'but the taxes are down,' and cited another number, say $3,442, 'Can you explain that to me?'

"I was simply amazed. I had heard that he had good common sense about law and business, but anything that was read to him, no matter how complicated it was, he could call it to mind and repeat it back to me perfectly."

Bobby also got to know Pat outside of the business world.

"At an annual meeting of the stockholders and senior club members one year, about 400 guys, we had a lobster buffet and then set up three gaming tables and rolled dice. The 'house' wasn't taking any money, so it was perfectly legal. I rolled for Pat and we all had a good time.

"He asked me to take him home uptown and so I did. We had a nightcap, then he fell asleep in his chair. Sherry was asleep, and I didn't know what to do, so I left him in his chair and went home.

"The next morning at 9:30 Pat called me, laughed and said, 'Okay you little SOB, I woke up this morning and didn't know where I was. I thought I was still at the club but didn't feel anything familiar. I was feeling around and found their phone, and called my house, but kept getting a busy signal. Then Sherry came down and said, 'Pat, what are you doing?' I told her I thought you had left me at the club!'

"He was a sharp businessman and always a great deal of fun to be with," Bobby continued, "because he never once, in the thirty years I knew him, complained about anything. Not about being blind or being dealt the short stick, nothing. Pat was the most positive person I ever met — the epitome of perseverance. He did everything like any other person would do and never complained once."

But of all the professions in which Pat Browne Jr. exceeded, none were more spectacularly well played than blind golf. The 1986 USBGA National Championship took place during October at the New Orleans Country Club, granting another chance to perform for the home folks. Forgotten was the painful loss there in 1973, all but erased by his 1980 championship won in New Orleans. Pat and Gerry had now won eight consecutive national championships and nine overall. Now at the top of his game and playing on his hometown course, Pat was brimming with confidence in 1986. But he hadn't forgotten those that had helped him rise to such heights.

He told *Times-Picayune* correspondent Richard Meek that blind golf coaches were sixty to seventy percent responsible for victories. He relied heavily on Gerry Barousse as coach, but when Gerry was unavailable, Ecole Classique High School golfer Jimmy Self Jr., Ole Miss golfer Chris Shuler, and Newman High School golfer Charles Monsted served as coaches.

Pat told Meek that he had been successful because he had better coaches than anyone else. "They have made the difference," he maintained.

Pat also said he had been working out on the Nautilus three days a week since he had recently played eleven courses in fourteen days and realized he had gotten out of shape. Now he could play the last few holes as well as he could play the first few.

He predicted that Joe Lazaro, Clarence McFarland, Charles Mayo and Eddie Erwin would be his main competition in the New Orleans tournament, yet he would be disappointed if he didn't win. "I've worked hard," he declared, "and prepared a long time."

In another *Times-Picayune* article published the same day, Pat evinced a reminiscent mood. He spoke to writer Dave Lagarde about his 1966 accident, recalling that the last thing he saw was a flashing blue light. He despaired of ever playing golf after the wreck until he read Charley Boswell's book, *Now I See*, that "triggered his interest in blind golf." He credited Joe Lazaro's book, *The Right Touch*, with helping him to cure a loop in his back swing. He opined that Boswell and Lazaro were primarily responsible for "starting what we have today" with blind golf. By that he meant that the most recent Guiding Eyes Classic tournament had raised $280,000 for training guide dogs for the blind.

The next day on October 11, Pat and Gerry shot a 98 for a first round lead over Clarence McFarland (103), Charles Mayo (107), while Eddie Erwin and Joe Lazaro tied for fourth at 116. Nevertheless, he declared that he had played poorly the first day. He said that the putter had been the problem and that he and Gerry were heading to the putting green to figure out what they had done wrong. Their chipping had not been ideal either. They had taken two triple-bogeys on the back nine, including one hole where he had taken two shots to get out of a bunker, and another triple-bogey caused by errant chipping. On the fourteenth hole they had three-putted from twenty-five feet.

"My score will improve," he predicted for his second round.

His competition had fared no better. Erwin had tens on two holes, Mayo suffered a ten, and Lazaro an eleven.

But Pat and Gerry did not improve the next day. They shot a 100 for a total of 198, but that was good enough to beat Joe Lazaro by ten strokes with his 208. Clarence McFarland shot a ten on the first hole and finished third with a 213 total.

Pat was again disappointed with his round before the home folks. "We worked hard," he told Meek, "and shot a 100. That's no good."

Even so, he had won his ninth straight championship and had done it again with friends and family watching. Only a perfectionist and intense competitor could be disappointed with anything to do with that, but Pat Browne was both of those.

The next year, Pat and Gerry traveled to Mount Kisco, New York to try to win their sixth consecutive and seventh overall Corcoran Cup title in the Guiding Eyes Classic at the 6,492-yard, par-71 Mount Kisco Country Club. The course had been designed in the 1920s by Scottish-born golf architect Tom Winston, known as the "peer of all links architects."

A links course is golf's oldest style, developed in Scotland along coastlines, and played on sandy soil. The fairways are often undulating, wide open spaces, pocked with sand dunes and grass bunkers, and pelted with high winds with few trees to slow those winds. American golfers usually play more parkland-style courses, built inland with many trees and lush grass as if they are strolling in a park. If parkland courses, like the New Orleans Country Club, say "pulchritude," links courses, such as Mount Kisco, scream "hold on to your hat!"

The club itself offered a unique history in several respects, not least for being named for an Algonquian chief. The club's first swimming pool had been fed by a continuously flowing stream originating from a pure spring, and featured a sand bottom and surrounding beach with Long Island sand. The current pool is located in the same location as the original.

Pat and Gerry continued their historic rise to blind golf fame by winning the 10th annual tournament by *eighteen* strokes over the second place finisher. They shot 97 while familiar foe Clarence MacFarland and his coach and wife, Marilyn, ended with 115 strokes.

Later that fall, Pat and Gerry brought home another USBGA title upon returning to Starmount Forest Country Club in Greensboro, North Carolina. Many might expect that winning two major tournaments for six years in a row would be the most significant sports accomplishment in the life of a fifty-three-year-old blind golfer. But the award that meant the most to Pat came the next year, and was one he had never even dreamed of winning.

On April 6, 1988, the *Times-Picayune* reported that the Golf Writers Association would name Pat Browne Jr. that year's recipient of the Ben Hogan Award, given to the golfer who overcame exceptional adversity. Past winners included President Eisenhower, Ken Venturi, now chairman of the Guiding Eyes Classic, professional golfers Gene Littler and Lee Trevino, as well as Charley Boswell and Joe Lazaro.

A grateful Pat Browne Jr. told *Times-Picayune* reporter Peter Finney that he considered receiving this award to be his greatest achievement in golf. Ben Hogan had been his idol and Browne had played the Oakland Hills course in Birmingham, Michigan, just after Hogan had won the 1951 U.S. Open there. Having just won the New Orleans City Junior Championship, he had taken on the course, making eleven putts on the back nine, but still shot 80. "Talk about a thrill," he said.

Not entirely satisfied, Pat then went to a Ben Hogan clinic and saw his idol perform in the flesh. Hogan amazed him, he said, by calling shots like fades and draws and then executing them just as he had said. "The guy shagging his balls didn't even have to move," Pat recalled.

He said that as a youth he never dreamed of touring as a professional golfer, and as a Tulane golfer, was only worried about being beaten by talented LSU golfers. In one tournament, he teed off with several of them on the first hole and hit his drive about 42 yards. To have won the Hogan Award was far beyond any of his youthful expectations.

In a reminiscing mood, Pat went on to tell Finney about his hole-in-one history. Last year, he related, he had used a four iron on a 169-yard par-3 hole at the San Francisco Golf Club. Pepe Colomes was coaching him and their shot landed two feet from the hole and rolled right in. Pepe shouted and lifted Pat into the air. "I was so excited I was a wreck," Pat said.

His first ace had come as a teenager playing at the New Orleans Country Club, where the prize for an ace was a fifth of Old Forrester. "I gave it to my dad," he said.

Time Magazine also reported that Pat was given the Ben Hogan Award in Augusta, Georgia, and recounted the time that Pat had been in the Master's gallery in 1967 when Hogan shot a 66. Asked in New Orleans how the event in Georgia went, Pat replied simply, "It was exciting."

Later that year Pat and Gerry won their seventh consecutive Corcoran Cup and the Guiding Eyes Classic in New York, and followed that with their eleventh straight USBGA National Championship in Coral Springs, Florida. There they fired an 87 and 90 for a 177 total on the Broken Wood Country Club course.

In 1989 they closed out their greatest decade so far by winning another championship at the Guiding Eyes Classic in New York before taking the USBGA National Championship in Au Clair, Wisconsin. In Wisconsin they fired a 41 on the front nine and a 50 on the back nine for a 91, finishing six shots ahead of their nearest competition. Rain washed out the second day, crowning them champions for yet another season.

Although Pat had enjoyed all the championships and working with his many coaches, he could not help wondering if someday his now ten-year-old son, Patrick III, would become his coach. First, of course, the boy would need to become an accomplished golfer in his own right.

"But Pat and I never pushed Patrick toward golf," Sherry said. "When he was eight he had started playing soccer, and that was the sport he loved more than golf while he was in school. He also loved basketball, and was very good although not tall like his father."

Former Ole Miss Rebels and New York Giants quarterback Eli Manning, who grew up in New Orleans and received his first golf lessons from Pat, remembers playing basketball with young Patrick. "We played against each other from different schools in junior high, but played together with the neighborhood team Carrollton Boosters, and won a championship one year.

"Patrick's dad loved golf and wanted Patrick to play with him, and later coach him," Eli recalled, "but he never pushed him to golf. His focus was on raising a good boy. That reminded me of my childhood. My dad didn't raise me to be a quarterback. He hoped I'd love it and I did love it on my own.

"The main thing Patrick learned from his dad," Eli

Eli Manning and Pat Browne Jr. in 2008, Mount Kisco, NY, Guiding Eyes Tournament won by Pat and his son Patrick and hosted by Eli Manning

continued, "was life lessons, especially a great attitude — how nothing ever got him down."

Eli's dad, Archie Manning, remembers those times the same way.

"Sure Pat wanted his son to play golf, but he didn't push it on him. He really loved 'Sheriff,' that's what he sometimes called Patrick."

One of Pat's coaches, David Clark, remembers much the same with regard to Patrick. "Pat was like a second father to me," Clark said, "and I saw first-hand how much he loved Patrick and his daughters. Sure, he wanted Patrick to play golf and coach him some day, but he never pushed him in that direction. He told me when Patrick was young that 'I sure hope Patrick takes up golf, but I won't force him.' He wanted most of all for Patrick to earn the right to be a leader in life as he himself had always been, and pushed him only in the right ways."

But Pat wondered, would doing it the right way be enough?

11

Taking the Show Across the Pond

In the end, it's still a game of golf, and if at the end of the day you can't shake hands with your opponents and still be friends, then you've missed the point.

— Payne Stewart

Count your age by friends, not years. Count your life by smiles, not tears.

— John Lennon

In early May 1990, Pat launched his golf highlights by playing the reigning PGA champion, Payne Stewart, in a nine-hole exhibition match at Walt Disney World's Lake Buena Vista course. Played to increase awareness of the blinding disease, retinitis pigmentosa, the exhibition yielded both a memorable contest and a wholesome respect from each golfer for the other.

Stewart gamely agreed to play blindfolded and shot a respectable 60, but Pat took the match by carding a 40.

"This was a humbling experience," Stewart said, "making me appreciate my eyesight even more. I hope it made people aware of the disease. It could happen to anyone. It might even happen to me one day."

A few days later, Stewart told a friend, "If I practiced every day I could never beat Pat Browne."

For his part, Pat had nothing but appreciation for the PGA champion, noting that he had been a great sport about it, and that few golfers of Stewart's stature would have made so much fun of themselves for such a good cause. Exhibiting the same high-spirited attitude after the exhibition, Pat said to the gracious Stewart, "Take that mask off and let me see what you look like."

Such events were always fun and right up the fun-

In 1983 with young Patrick, wearing knickers sent to him by Payne Stewart

loving Pat Browne's alley, but sooner or later, the specter of hard-fought tournaments would raise its gnarly head every year. As always, however, Pat and Gerry were ready for the 1990 Guiding Eyes Classic in Mount Kisco that year, winning yet another Corcoran Cup, their ninth consecutive victory there, and their tenth overall.

The August 1990 USBGA Championship at the Lake Buena Vista course in Orlando would also be serious business, although never so serious that the participants couldn't pass a good time with the press. Golfer Worth Dalton of Winter Springs, Florida, had been a two-sport athlete in high school who lost his sight at age thirty-three from retinitis pigmentosa. He too, had defeated a blindfolded Payne Stewart in an exhibition designed to raise money for finding a cure for the disease that blinded him.

Yet while preparing to play the USBGA tournament, he took the time to exhibit some of the brand of humor for which many blind golfers were well known. He informed *Times-Picayune* sportswriter Dave Lagarde that he had a "plan to beat Pat Browne this year. We're going to get to Gerry Barousse," he declared, his tongue planted firmly in his cheek. "Pat would be lost without him, as would be any sightless golfer without his coach."

"There are a half dozen guys capable of beating Pat," Dalton added. "But only if they're on and he's off."

The chances of Pat being off were slim at that time, as he had been playing daily with coaches Gerry Barousse, Charles Monsted and Jamie Christovich. He'd also been taking lessons from New Orleans Country Club professional Gordon Johnson, who had been attempting to get Pat to use his whole body on his swing and not just his arms and hands. When he took Johnson's advice, Pat noted, it added "fifteen yards to his drives."

As always, Pat kept things in perspective. "We're really excited about going to Disney World," he told Lagarde. "I think it will help us get our message out," he said, referring to the need to raise awareness of retinitis pigmentosa.

All the hard work apparently paid off for Pat and Gerry, as they bested eighteen other teams to capture their 14th USBGA title and their 13th consecutive win. Although rain shortened the tournament to twenty-seven holes, Pat shot a 133 to beat Dave Meador (157) by twenty-four strokes. Charles Mayo finished third with a 159. Once again Pat had been on and the rest of the field considerably off in the face of such fierce competition.

Three months later, *Times-Picayune* social scene writer Nell Nolan penned an article that revealed much about how "the other half" partied in New Orleans. The New Orleans Country Club Board of Governors threw a fundraiser supporting the local branch of the Volunteer and Information Agency, and Board President Pat Browne Jr. and his wife Sherry greeted the revelers along with other governors including Gerry Barousse.

It proved quite a feast and Nolan reported that the fare included appetizers of boiled shrimp, smoked salmon, stuffed pea pods, cheese puffs and cocktails. Dinner included a first course of crab cakes with a "fresh tomato sauce," followed by "quail in a potato nest" and chateaubriand, with "peach ice cream in an edible chocolate cup" for dessert.

Adding a touch of wit to her description, Nolan said that "more color was provided by Sherry Browne's red

Pat as New Orleans Country Club president, wearing the club green jacket in which he would be buried

top and black skirt, which belied both her names."

Another *Times-Picayune* writer, Angus Lind, penned an article, "A Driving Force," on March 22, 1991, that noted some of Pat's key accomplishments as well as his penchant for "slipping in subtle one-liners frequently aimed at his [sightless] lifestyle."

Lind reported that Browne had crafted two holes-in-one, something one half of one percent of all golfers had ever achieved. In June of 1990 Pat had shot a 35 at his home club with an eagle on the par-4 16th hole and holing out on his second shot with a three iron. Lind also reported that Pat had once shot a 76 on his home course and 91 at the Masters course in Augusta. In 1982 at the USBGA Championship in Greensboro, he carded a 36 on the back nine in one round, the first time that had ever been accomplished in blind golf.

As for the champ's unique blend of sense of humor, Lind relayed several prime examples. "I never fooled much with braille," Pat had observed, "except to learn enough to play gin rummy."

Pat told him that learning to "listen intently" was an advantage for him, but also a necessity since all communication for him was the spoken word. "Paying attention was easier," he continued, "because you don't get distracted if there's some good-looking woman around."

Finally, Lind observed that coming to the end of a recent round of golf, Pat asked his sighted companion, "Is it light enough for a couple more (holes)?"

Perhaps Pat's sense of humor was as important a part of his winning ways as was his faith, because nothing seemed to take him off the path to victory after victory. Later that year Pat continued his championship winning ways, defeating Dave Meador and Joe Lazaro in the June, 1991 Guiding Eyes Classic and winning his 10th straight and 11th overall Corcoran Cup. That fall, Pat and Gerry traveled to Walt Disney World's Lake Buena Vista course where all USBGA Championship tournaments were now played, and won their 13th straight and 14th overall national championship.

Although it appeared that Pat and Gerry were ensconced on the summit of the blind golf world and unbeatable wherever they played, they were about to discover the truism that golf always presents new challenges, even when you believe you've arrived at the top of your game.

In 1992 another of Pat's dreams came true. Back in 1979 he had first hoped that someday British golfers would vie with their American counterparts for some form of world cup of blind golf. Or as he had said, "Before I get too old." With that thought in mind, Pat had worked hard to make that happen, contacting England's Blind Golf Society in 1995 with his idea to set up just such a match.

The British had agreed to play in 1991, but with a major stipulation—while the American golfers would all be entirely sightless, their British opponents could include legally blind but not entirely sightless players capable of light perception. This was presumably due to a lack of completely blind golfers of Pat's and his American cohort's abilities.

The 1992 match pitted four, two-man American teams against four, two-man British teams, with each match being worth one point. The match was played at Wentworth Country Club just outside London. It featured match play, rather than the stroke play utilized in American national championships. In stroke play you count the number of strokes. In match play you count the number of holes won.

Pat knew he was not too old, but his handicap had risen from a two in college, to a fifteen before the accident, to a seventeen in recent years, and a nineteen in 1992. In the end, the odds proved too much for him and the Americans, as the British won easily, 10-2, claiming the world's first Rainbow Cup. Pat was shut out in his matches.

Pat and Gerry would have to wait a full year before taking another shot at the British, but they didn't waste their time worrying about it. In the spring of 1992 they won another Corcoran Cup at the Guiding Eyes Classic in Mount Kisco, and in the fall they claimed another USBGA National Championship in Orlando on Disney's Lake Buena Vista Course.

In the latter tournament, Pat shot a 95, besting by twelve strokes the last man to beat him in the tournament back in 1977. Dave Meador finished second with a 107. Rain washed out the second day, but couldn't prevent Pat and Gerry from winning their 15th straight blind golf championship, or stop them from copping two major tournaments in the same year one more time.

In 1993, they again won both majors, with the win in Orlando leaving no doubt who ruled blind golf in America. Pat vanquished his old foe, second place finisher Dave Meador, in the Daiwa USBGA National Championship by a whopping twenty-seven stroke margin, 188 to 215.

"Gerry did a good job," Pat told *Times-Picayune* sports editor Dave Lagarde, "I hit a lot of good shots and kept the ball in play. Now we look to the Stewart Cup," he concluded pointedly. The Rainbow Cup had been renamed upon the move to America in 1993, in honor of Frank Stewart Jr., the owner of Stewart Enterprises in New Orleans, and sponsor of the tournament.

Indeed, the match with the British was the one Pat had been gunning for all year. He knew the British were coming in September—coming not only to America, but to Pat's home course, The New Orleans Country Club. This time the match featured two, eight-man teams and two days of match play. Pat told Dave Lagarde that he was well aware that the Americans had been routed the year before, and that despite the home field advantage, they had their "hands full again."

Certain American players were selected for winning the USBGA national championship, the Guiding Eyes Classic, and the Heather Farr Drive for Sight Classic, while others were chosen because they were among the best to be had. At New Orleans, the American team would include Pat as captain, and three of his old friends and adversaries, Charles Mayo, Joe Lazaro and Dave Meador.

During the days before the international event, Pat told *Times-Picayune* staff writer Ted Lewis how serious he was about the upcoming match. "We're playing for the United States," he declared. "You don't get to represent your country very often. So we mean business."

The first day of the tournament, September 11, Pat and Jim Baker defeated David Morris and Roy McKnight 7-5, winning the first five holes with pars and halving the next five. They won the next two holes to wrap up their match.

It's always nice to know your partner is down the middle every time," Baker told Lewis. "He and Gerry had the home field advantage."

British opponent David Morris was even more succinct. "There was nothing we could do," he said. Then he added, "Pat's the best player in the world, and what he did his partner did."

The second day, Bob Andrews, who had been blinded by a booby trap in Vietnam, led the Americans to victory with a 3-2 win over Graham Salms. Pat, Dave Meador, Jim Baker, Walter Deitz and Worth Dalton also prevailed in their individual matches, as the Americans repaid the British with a rout of their own.

Pat whipped David Morris again, this time 5-3, making use of three birdies.

While Pat exclaimed that the only thing better would have been a clean sweep, Morris predicted that his team's play would be better the next year in Britain.

On September 29, Pat, Sherry, Gerry, and his wife Jeanne were feted as international champions at the Rotary Club's awards dinner at the Fairmont Hotel.

As always, Pat did not let another year go by without making yet another stand in support of charitable causes. In October he served as Master of Ceremony at a rally celebrating Louisiana's White Cane Safety Laws for the blind and visually impaired. Those laws were in place throughout the country, but with slightly different provisions and punishments for violations depending upon the state.

In Louisiana, drivers were required to stop ten feet from any pedestrian carrying a white cane or using a guide dog in or near an intersection or roadway. Only the blind or visually impaired were allowed to carry white canes in those locations. Fines for violating those laws included a $175 fine and no more than thirty days in jail for a first office, and $500 and no more than ninety days for any subsequent convictions.

Pat had accomplished almost everything he had set out to accomplish years earlier, both in golf and in life, and in support of those who had endured endless darkness as he had. But as it does with all champions of any kind, that eternal predator time was closing in on him, and even his skills would start to wane as he reached his golden years.

He and Gerry continued to win the USBGA National Championship every year through 1997, and Pat would win the Guiding Eyes Classic Corcoran Cup every year through 1997, often with Gerry, but in 1995 and 1997, with David Clarke.

Such achievements drew national and international interest with both the press and golf fans everywhere. Nike included a photo of Pat and Gerry in their first print "Just Do It" ad. Bryant and Greg Gumbel also did a piece on him. In June of 1994, Pat appeared on ABC's *Nightline* with Ted Koppel.

In a *Nightline* segment entitled "Golf Stories," Pat was one of three golfers covered for their unusual skills. In his story, Pat related how much he wanted to come back and play golf after his accident, and to know if he could do it again. Once he hit it well, he told *Nightline,* he was hooked.

Pat's segment showed him playing golf with the aid of his coach, Gerry Barousse. As always Pat stated that having a coach position him on the course was the hard part, and that the "easy part was to swing the club." Interviewed on his home course, the New Orleans Country Club, Pat said his best round there had been a 78, that he played three tournaments a year, and none of that would have been possible without Gerry Barousse, the greatest blind golf coach ever. "You'll always hear me say, 'we won,'" he said, adding that he believed there should always be two names on every blind golf championship trophy.

He also told a humorous story about the time he was practicing in his home with 7 iron and damaged the wall severely, so that he and Sherry ultimately got a new kitchen.

Pat concluded the interview as he often did, giving credit where he believed credit was due, even for things that at first seemed more an unmitigated disaster than a blessing. If not for his blindness, he maintained, he would never have been more than a weekend golfer. But now he traveled the world playing golf, "so the Lord knew what he was doing."

All the publicity was a sweet lagniappe for Pat, and a major shot in the arm for blind golf and the money it could raise for the blind, but for all his accomplishments and unbridled optimism, there were hints that Pat might be finally slowing down. In 1994 at the USBGA championship in Orlando, he and Gerry beat second place finisher Joe Lazaro by only eight strokes, their smallest margin of victory in ten years. More significantly, that proved their 17th consecutive championship, their 18th overall, outstripping Pat's old friend Charley Boswell's record of 17 total national championship victories, making them the greatest team in the history of blind golf.

That slowing trend continued in September 1995, at the Pat Shull Park Golf and Country Club in Pattingham, Shropshire, England, where the British team soundly whipped Pat and the Americans, 11-1.

Even so, it was time to honor New Orleans' and the world's greatest blind golf champion and humanitarian as only denizens of the Crescent City could do. In March of 1996 Pat was one of five people admitted to the Greater New Orleans Sports Hall of Fame. In October his name was carved on the Hilton Riverside Hotel sidewalk for being inducted into the Walk of Fame, alongside fellow inductees former Governor Edwin Edwards, Irma Strode, long-time captain of the venerable Carnival Krewe of Iris, and international entertainer Phil Harris. World Famous New Orleans musician Pete Fountain entertained at the event, having been previously chosen for the award himself.

The year 1997 saw the second annual Israel/Aron Tulane Classic Tournament held at Lakewood Golf Club in honor of Pat Browne Jr., and he would be elected to the Louisiana Sports Hall of Fame the very next year. After that induction Pat told his son that, "If I have accomplished anything at all, it's that the struggles I went through helped me to take on many challenges and succeed. And if I helped one person whose life forced him to struggle as I did, that was worth more than any number of championships I won."

But just as it seemed that life was slowing down the sixty-three-year-old Pat Browne Jr., life threw him another curve. At this crossroads, fighting health problems as well as age, he was about to be challenged to the core of his being once more. And again, it would either plunge him into the depths of despair or raise him to unprecedented heights of ecstasy.

Would Pat Browne Jr. rise to that occasion?

12

A Chip Off the Old Block

You can't help getting older, but you don't have to get old.
—George Burns

Never let the fear of striking out keep you from coming up to bat. It's hard to beat a person who never gives up.
—Babe Ruth

In 1997, Pat won the Guiding Eyes Classic, but not with Gerry Barousse. David Clarke had coached him to that victory, as he had done in 1995. Having won championships with several excellent young coaches, Pat began thinking ever more seriously about winning one with his son Patrick.

This had been on his mind since 1981, when Patrick was born. Once the boy entered high school in 1996, the idea rarely ever left Pat's mind. He fervently hoped Patrick would acquire a love of golf and then become accomplished in the sport. But Patrick had favored other sports early on, particularly soccer and football in elementary school and basketball in junior high.

Entering Jesuit High School in 1996, Patrick tried out for the football team but barely missed the cut. It was then that he decided to take up golf.

"We were riding home from the tryout," Patrick said, "and Dad was worrying that he had pushed me to go to Jesuit where he had gone, and that if he hadn't I could have played football or basketball at any of the other New Orleans high schools. I suddenly announced that I was glad to be at Jesuit and I was going to focus on golf. I was driving and couldn't see him, but Mom saw him give a celebratory fist pump."

This was great news for Pat but raised many questions all the same. Would Patrick enjoy the game like he did? Would he become proficient enough to win tournaments on his own, much less be able to coach his father in national championship tournaments? And even if he could, by the time Patrick was ready to coach, would Pat still have the ability to win a national title? He was sixty-four now and would be sixty-eight by the time Patrick graduated high school. And in his mid-seventies when Patrick finished college.

And there was always the nagging thought that wouldn't leave him alone whenever he considered the Patrick question—he had wanted so badly to win a national championship for his father but had thrown away his last chance and folded on the final hole in 1972. Was he fated to repeat that failure with his son even if the chance came his way?

Perhaps that thought was on his mind when he and David Clarke traveled to Mount Kisco in the spring of 1997 for another shot at the Guiding Eyes Classic. They won the tournament with relative ease, and Pat was well aware that David, like Gerry, was a more than a proficient golfer.

David Clarke had played college golf, then took a shot at the Pro-Am tour, but within two years had realized that he was "not PGA caliber." He then became an assistant golf pro in Mobile, where he met Pat in 1989. Pat owned a condo in Point Clear and played at the Lakewood Golf

Club when in town and also at the Grand Hotel course in nearby Mobile.

"I saw him on a practice range with Gerry Barousse," David recalled, "hitting 250-yard drives right down the middle. After we met I often helped him practice when he came to Point Clear. Years later I began coaching him at the Guiding Eyes Classic in New York when Gerry or Charles Monsted were unavailable.

"We won in 1995, but then I became the first coach to help him lose the Classic in 1996. We made up for it by winning the tournament in 1997 by twenty strokes. That was my proudest moment in golf. He didn't play in 1998 because his back was hurting him.

"The thing about Pat," David said, "was that he realized that win or lose it was a team sport, and that he couldn't do anything without his coach. And he was really waiting for his son to become a scratch golfer so Patrick could coach him in the Guiding Eyes Classic."

"Before it was too late," David did not say, but the subject of age is one that haunts all great athletes when their time comes around. Yet there were no fiercer competitors than blind golfers, those who had always refused to let anything stop them from competing. "Pat was never going to give up until he had accomplished what he wanted," David said.

That was certainly the case with seventy-nine-year-old Joe Lazaro who was preparing to challenge Pat later that year in the 1997 Daiwa USBGA National Championship in September at the Lake Buena Vista golf course in Orlando. On August 10th, the *Times-Picayune New Orleans States Item* ran an AP story off the wire that had found Lazaro preparing for that tournament and remembering the events that had set him on his path.

He recounted the story of how he was blinded in WWII as a member of a mine detection team near Florence, Italy. A nearby jeep hit a mine and "It was like hell exploded," Lazaro recalled. "I felt like I had a bucket of fire thrown in my face. I was flipped back like a chicken thrown off a stone wall."

Yet for all the horror and pain, Joe had felt fortunate to be alive. "What if I had been in that jeep?" he said.

Turning to the tournament, he reckoned he would once again face his old friend and combatant, Pat Browne Jr. He was going to stop Pat's streak at 19 straight in Orlando next month, he predicted.

Appraised of his friend's prediction, Pat said, "That's typical Joe. He plays just as hard now as when I first met him in 1969." Observing that his friend had never grown resentful about either his wartime injury or becoming permanently blind, Pat related that Joe had moved on with his life, and his young wife "had stayed with him and given him three children."

Whatever concerns about growing old or playing with his son were on Pat's mind at that time, no one would have known it. Pat and Gerry won their twenty-first USBGA National Championship, their twentieth in a row by their widest margin to date.

"That makes it kind of special," said Pat, who shot a 91 and 88 for a total of 179 on the 36-hole affair, finishing 45 strokes ahead of second place finisher Dave Meador.

The combination of age and back problems would nevertheless sideline Pat the next year, making the 1997 national championship victory his last in eight years. The Guiding Eyes Classic was still on his radar, however, and, whether with Gerry, David or Charles, he would still be a force to reckon with in the battle for the Corcoran Cup for the next decade.

And with Pat, there was always time for hijinks along the way.

"Pat put on a lot of clinics during that time," David Clarke recalled. "He would demonstrate a 20 or 40 foot putt" with his Callaway Bobby Jones putter. "I'd walk him from his ball to the pin so he could get a feel for the slope and distance. Then I'd tell him something like, it's uphill for ten feet then the last thirty feet are downhill. He'd say, 'That's brutal, Pro.' He always called me 'Pro.' He'd miss a few, always coming close, then sink one of those long putts, and the gallery would erupt with cheers. Then he'd say, 'Well, that's it, I can't do any better than that,' wave to the crowd, and walk off! They loved it.

"So did the press," David continued. "CNN interviewed him, as did *Nightline,* and Bryant and Greg Gumbel. When we were in England a BBC reporter followed him around on the course.

"But he thought continuing to play in the Guiding Eyes tournament was very important. He really liked the event chairman, Ken Venturi, a former Masters champion, and of course winning it was important. But he had insisted that the winning coaches' names be on the Corcoran Cup trophies along with the winning players, and when we won in 1999, he even gave me the trophy itself."

"But again, it wasn't even winning that was most important to Pat. He helped raise tens of millions to train guide dogs for the blind. He knew it cost thirty-five thousand to train each dog, and he was committed to doing his part.

"And win or lose," David continued, "either way he

was a good Christian person, and whenever we were playing a tournament the first thing he did when we got into town was find a restaurant and church near the course, and he never failed to go to mass that weekend. He was the greatest person I've ever known."

David also remembered Pat's great sense of humor and penchant for playing jokes on others. "Once I took him to his condo after a round at Lakewood in Point Clear," David said. "His elevator was in his garage, and his condo was on the third floor. He got his clubs and went into the elevator with me, then switched off all the lights, and said, "Now we're even you little SOB!""

The joke was sometimes on Pat, though. "Once," David related, "it began raining on the Dogwood Hills course in Hattiesburg, and we walked toward a six-foot-tall shed near the 16th green. I'm 5' 9" and Pat is 6' 4" so he followed me into the shed, his hand on my shoulder as always, and hit his head on the roof when I didn't warn him. With his hand on my shoulder he moved so well I sometimes forgot he was blind."

But though he was blind, David noted, "he didn't have any difficulty seeing into his friend's hearts and minds. He might say to me, 'Pro, you seem distracted today,' but he never was. He liked to say that he was always 'dialed in' to everyone and everything around him. He was highly intelligent and intuitive. Always saying that his greatest gift was to listen."

Archie Manning remembers Pat's dialed-in ability well. "He recognized everyone by voice," Archie said. "I wouldn't see him for a while and then run into him on the course or in the clubhouse and I'd say hello, and he would always say, 'Hey Archie.' He always knew who he was talking to."

If Pat was dialed-in to everyone he met, he was certainly well aware of the progress his son Patrick was making on the links. In 1997 Patrick played on the Jesuit High golf team that barely lost the state championship in his sophomore year. Jesuit won the state championship Patrick's junior and senior years, and his play had been instrumental in garnering those wins.

On April 28, 1999, *Times-Picayune* staff writer Pierce Huff reported that Patrick shot 3 over par (75) for a one-shot victory in his match to lead the Jesuit golf team to its third consecutive regional title at the Lakewood Country Club course in Algiers. Like his father, Patrick was quick to give credit where he believed it was due.

Watching his father, the Jesuit senior told Huff, taught him that there were "few obstacles that couldn't be overcome with hard work and mental toughness." This was a reference to the high wind that had kicked up on the back nine that Patrick was able to play through to victory. "Dad had broken almost everything in the car wreck" that had blinded him, Patrick continued, noting that many people may have given up at that point, "but he didn't." His dad had coached him on the mental game, going over all his shots after matches. "He helped me out a lot," Patrick concluded.

Patrick had shot a final round of 37 and 38 that included two birdies, five bogeys and eleven pars. "I was pretty pleased with what I did," he said, "maneuvering" his ball, hitting it low into the wind, especially on the back nine which had played much harder. The final tally showed that the Jesuit team carded a 306, good enough to best Brother Martin by 17 strokes.

One month later the Jesuit golfers won their second

straight Division 1 state title at Gemstone Plantation Golf Course. The boys had bettered their first round score by 31 strokes to take the title, and after the win, tossed coach Robin Hanemann into one of the course's lakes.

Patrick enjoyed those times immensely, but it was the quality times he spent with his father that really meant the most. "Around that time," he recalled, "I was taking some golf lessons from Hank Johnson, a celebrated instructor in Birmingham at Greystone Golf and Country Club. It was a five-hour drive and Dad would often come along with me. We would talk about life in general, and I would ask him how he overcame his difficulties, how he maintained his faith through it all. He really opened his heart to me, saying how truly thankful he was for his difficulties, and how they made him such a stronger person than he had ever known he could be. He said he felt he had been given a second chance in life, to start a second family. How meeting my mom was such an extraordinary life-changing event, and how it gave him a chance to have his only son at the older age of forty-eight. He told me how much I meant to him too, and how thankful he was for me."

Patrick also remembered the time his father invited him to lunch at his favorite men's club in New Orleans, the Louisiana Club, and surprised Patrick with his induction into the club. The tradition was for the new member to pay for drinks for everyone, but so many of Pat's friends had come to see it happen, that he treated everyone. Most stayed till 6:00 pm, but after that, the staff left us the keys and Dad and I stayed there till 10:00 pm celebrating. We took a cab home, and Mom met us at the door. She was so excited about my induction and the way they had surprised me, if not quite as excited about the condition we were in when we got home!"

But inevitably, the time for golf rolled back around. Patrick's play at Jesuit had convinced Pat that his son was ready to coach him at the Guiding Eyes tournament. When Patrick agreed, they were ready to take their shot two months later in June 1999.

Remembering his failure to win a championship for his dad may have interfered with his play, as Pat finished third with a 107, four strokes behind Dave Meador and Keith Melick of Longwood, Florida. Melick, coached by his wife Jean, won the first playoff hole to gain the Corcoran Cup.

Unfortunately for the new father and son team, Melick won the Guiding Eyes Classic the next three years. The succeeding three years saw the Corcoran Cup go to either Phil Blackwell and coach Rod Turnage, or Dave Meador and coach Everett Davis. In 2003, for example, Pat and Patrick finished third, eight strokes behind Phil Blackwell and coach Rod Turnage.

In 2001, Gerry Barousse coached Pat to a third place finish, so not all those losses came with Patrick as his coach. But six of those losses had, and this had hit Pat very hard. Part of the problem was his back which continued to plague him, but he often fell apart on the final holes, perhaps because he wanted so badly to win with his son.

The tension fell off a little when the father and son duo took time every year to participate in the Pat Browne Radio For the Blind Tournament, a charitable annual event played in New Orleans in tribute to Pat and to raise money for blind and vision- impaired people.

During those events, Pat and Patrick would set up on a par 3 tee box and challenge all comers to Beat Pat's Shot. Challengers had to pay a charitable $20 fee and wear a blindfold for a chance to gain the distinction of besting the world's greatest blind golfer by coming closest to the pin.

"I don't remember anyone ever doing it over the years with hundreds and hundreds of takers," Patrick laughed. "They had a better chance of receiving a prize given by Eli Manning for hitting the longest drive on the day."

Finally, Pat and Patrick got another chance to win a championship together, but this would be the most difficult challenge they would ever face. It came at the 2005 USBGA National Championship Tournament in Raleigh, North Carolina in September of that year.

With Patrick, putting in Raleigh, North Carolina in 2005, their first Blind Golf National Championship won together as a father-and-son team

The challenge there was two-fold. First, the Wildwood Green Country Club was a very hilly course, the kind that always gave Pat difficulty. This was so because uphill and downhill lies caused serious balance issues for blind golfers, and Pat was no exception. Golfers know that if the ball is on a hill and below their feet, the ball will curve left to right and, being a fade, will not have the same distance as a regular shot. A ball above their feet will curve right to left, and being a draw, will travel farther than would a fade. It's a question of picking a longer hitting club on the fade and a shorter club on the draw. That's difficult enough for most golfers, but blind golfers face a serious challenge in not tumbling down the hill every time they take those shots.

"Second, my father was putting enormous pressure on himself to win one with his son. He had failed to do so for his terminally ill father, and he knew that with his age and declining health, this would likely be his last opportunity to win the national championship tournament.

Patrick explained the problem caused by the added pressure. "Each year we lost made winning the next year all the more difficult. We would put so much pressure on ourselves, that despite the fact that we were more prepared than the other teams and had worked so much harder than most of them, we would struggle coming out the gate and put ourselves in such a deep hole with double and triple bogeys that we simply couldn't catch up on the last few holes. Or we would start strong and then struggle at the end. We let the pressure build up so high that anytime we had a hiccup, a double bogey or worse, the wheels would completely come off. Dad would hit terrible shots he hadn't hit all year, and we would find a way to lose.

"So I decided," Patrick recalled, "that I had to become Dad's psychiatrist, and find a way to get him get over the hump. After all, we had more advantages than most teams and shouldn't have had so much difficulty. Number one, Dad was clearly the greatest blind golfer of all time, and had won many championships before. Two, I was a college golfer and toyed with the idea of going pro, just as had been the case with many of his coaches in previous years. Many of the other golfers didn't have coaches who were also near scratch golfers themselves; often family members or at best local club pros who were in the twilight of their careers. All of Dad's coaches knew the game, could read the greens, and understand the speed of different greens with different grass and cuts.

"So," Patrick continued, "we had our biggest advantage

on the greens. The other golfers simply couldn't compete with him on the greens. So if we could avoid hazards and other big mistakes on the way to the green, we would usually take the hole.

"Most other coaches would simply say, 'It's a 10-foot putt that breaks about a foot to the right.' Our system was far more complex and helpful to my father. We would take two-foot-long steps on the green, his hand on my shoulder, and walk along the curve of the green. If it was a 12-foot putt uphill, he could feel that. A line with a break is longer than straight to the hole, so after he felt the break, I would tell him to swing as if it was a 14-foot putt, and then watch his practice strokes and tell him when he had the right stroke to go the needed distance. Then he'd put it in the hole. We rarely ever took more than one or two strokes to get it in the hole, while many other teams struggled with three or four putts.

"Another key point was that the golfer and coach were a real team, and after they had practiced and played together for years, as Dad did with Gerry Barousse, they could almost read each other's minds. The coach knew which instructions to give, and the golfer knew exactly what he meant when he said it.

"By 2005 we had played together long enough to be that kind of team, and we were determined to get the monkey off our backs. But I knew what was at stake for him that year. It was win this one or he would remember the failure for the rest of his life, just as he had when he failed to win one for his father."

One thing that worked in their favor was that this year's tournament was a rare two-day affair, rather than a three-day event with three days of pressure to overcome. This meant that if they could get off to a good start and take a sizable lead, they'd only have one more day to hold the line.

And that's precisely how it turned out. "We played a solid round the first day," Patrick declared, "then we managed the course well the next day, avoided the triple bogeys, and held on to our big lead. In 2005, Dad and I were the USBGA national champions, and I can't tell you how excited we were, and how excited Mom was to finally see us win the big one."

They lost the 2006 Guiding Eyes Tournament and

At the 2005 National Championship won by Pat and Patrick, with their trophies that Pat insisted go to coaches as well as players

wondered if they were going to be a flash in the pan, one and gone.

Looming in the back of their minds throughout 2007 was an upcoming major tournament in the state of New York, the one that had bedeviled them every time they had attempted it together.

But in June of 2007, Pat's back felt much better, he was swinging his Big Bertha golf clubs well, and he believed that he and Patrick would have their best chance yet to emblazon their names on the Corcoran Cup. And as fate would have it, that year, the 30th Annual Guiding Eyes Classic would be hosted by the Brownes' good friend, Eli Manning, at the Whippoorwill Golf Club in Armonk, New York.

Prior to the tournament, Pat and Eli played a warm-up round together, during which Eli noted that his seventy-four-year old friend was still "unbelievable" despite his age, and that Pat and Patrick were working well together.

"It was like when we played a few holes years before in New Orleans," Eli continued. "He made it look so easy then, and not a lot had changed over the years. Whenever he hit a bad shot, he kept a great attitude about it. And he loved the competition, just as Patrick did. But even though he won the Guiding Eyes many times, he was always humble about it, never really talked about it. To me, these were some of the reasons why he was still winning championships in his seventies," Eli concluded.

For his part, Eli was very pleased to be participating as host for the Guiding Eyes Classic for the same reason that Pat continued to play there. "I got involved in Guiding Eyes," Eli recounted, "because of Pat. He had helped raise a lot of money to provide guide dogs for free,

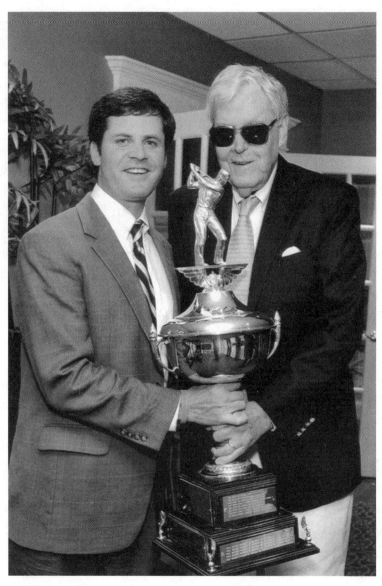

Guiding Eyes Tournament won by Pat and Patrick in 2007

Guiding Eyes Tournament, 2007, with Patrick, Sherry, and host Eli Manning, won by Pat and Patrick

which completely changed many people's lives. I've seen firsthand the way it has changed lives, and, like Pat, I've always been thankful to be a part of that."

That same year, the community-minded Eli would undertake a five-year campaign to raise $2.5 million dollars for the construction of the Eli Manning Children's Clinics at the Blair E. Batson Hospital for Children in Jackson, Mississippi. Along with receiving numerous humanitarian awards, the world champion quarterback would go on to lend his support to multiple charities such as the March of Dimes, Boys and Girls Clubs of America and the Red Cross. He remains the host of the Guiding Eyes Classic to this day.

And although the charitable aspect of the Guiding Eyes

New York City 2006, from left to right: Mr. and Mrs. Bill Badger, Eli and Abby Manning, Pat and Patrick, kicking off a Guiding Eyes fundraising for the blind event

Classic had always been foremost on the minds of Pat, Eli, and Patrick every year, 2007 brought a motivation to Pat Browne Jr. that, if only for one year, may have taken precedence over any others.

"Pat really wanted to win that tournament with Patrick," Eli recalled, "but I'm not sure he was as worried about that as Patrick was. Patrick really didn't want to be the weak link in his father's coaching chain. But they both approached it in a loving way; they wanted to win it for each other most of all."

That the winning players and coach's names were added to the trophy every year made winning it all the more significant to the father and son. No number of Corcoran trophies in Pat's trophy case could make up for the lack of one with Pat and Patrick's names side-by-side.

Years earlier, Pat had insisted that the coach's name should appear on the trophy alongside the winning golfer's name. As Eli's father, Archie Manning, had always said, "No quarterback has ever won a championship by himself." Pat Browne Jr. had always echoed that sentiment when he declared after winning each national championship that "You'll never hear me say, 'I' won the championship. It's always 'we' won."

Now, Pat's desire to see his son's name on that trophy had become extreme, and Patrick's wish to see his father's name on the 2007 Corcoran Cup was just as strong.

But could they do it? They had failed numerous times, but having won the national championship together,

Guiding Eyes Tournament, 2007, won with Patrick, Mount Kisco, NY

they felt confident they'd get this one in the bag too. And so they did, winning their first Guiding Eyes Classic together.

With the win, Pat had accomplished almost everything he had set out to accomplish in blind golf, and for most champions, especially those in their 70's suffering bad backs, this championship with his son's name on the trophy would have been an admirable way to go out.

And the back was not the only problem. Sarasota golf coach Joe McCourt noticed around this time that Pat's right hand had begun to shake a little when he took hold of the club's shaft, but when he took the club back to swing, the shaking ceased entirely.

But nothing was going to shake Pat's desire to keep winning with Patrick, now that they had shown they could do it. They lost the Guiding Eyes championship in 2009 but came back to win once more in 2010. The next year, Pat would play for the Corcoran Cup with another coach, Charles Monsted. They had won the Guiding Eyes together in 1985 and 1986, but the 2011 tournament presented challenges they hadn't faced back then. Pat was decades older and suffering from back problems, and his handicap had slipped more than a few strokes. Charles hadn't played with Pat in a championship tournament since the mid 80s, and they hadn't had much time to reacquaint themselves when Patrick discovered at the last second that he would be unavailable to coach his father.

Charles Monsted was now a family man and a successful businessman in sales and marketing, and it was not as easy now as it had been in college to pick up, leave his responsibilities behind, and head off to New York to play golf.

Pat and coach Charles Monsted, 2006, by Pat's home in Uptown New Orleans

But there was something about playing with Pat, Charles noted, that put everyone at ease no matter the circumstance.

"Pat was the most competitive man I ever met," Charles continued, "but you wouldn't know it if you hadn't played a sport with him. He was so easy going, and took every hardship or loss with such aplomb, that you would think that all he cared about were his friends and family, and that golf meant nothing to him. But nothing could have been further from the truth.

"I truly admired the man." Charles said. "This is a man who never blamed anyone for anything that went wrong, gave all the credit to his coaches when he won, and thanked God every day for the life he had enjoyed. And this is the same man who was broken up and blinded in a car wreck, who had seen his life go completely down the drain, and yet never gave up. You can't help but do whatever needs doing to help that man win. And you can believe that I did."

So when the 2011 Guiding Eyes Classic rolled around, Eli Manning once again hosted the men who had recently won the Cup (Phil Blackwell [2001, 2003, 2004, 2006, 2008] and Dave Meador [2005, 2009]) teed it up again, only to see Charles and Pat take the Corcoran Cup one more time.

Playing with Patrick the next year (2012), Pat took home another Guiding Eyes Classic trophy, but it would be the last major he would ever win. But oh, what a career he had enjoyed, making himself the greatest blind golfer of all time and winning several majors with his son as a coach. It had been a long climb from the hole he found himself in back in 1966, enveloped in darkness and not even able to get out of his hospital bed for several months.

Turnberry Course, Scotland, 9th hole fairway, with his son and coach, Patrick

Pat and Patrick at Turnberry, Scotland

Mount Kisco, NY, Guiding Eyes Championship 2012, with Patrick as coach, 18th green after putting out to win

But Pat Browne Jr. had done it, and while doing it, he never once bragged about his accomplishments, gave all the credit to his coaches, thanked God for giving him the strength to do it, and remained a humble, charitable, loving family man and boon companion to his friends. Who could argue that these are the marks of a true sports champion and make an ideal blueprint for a life well played?

13

LEAVING A MIRACULOUS LEGACY

Out of difficulties grow miracles.
                —French philosopher Jean de la Bruyere

Carve your name on hearts, not tombstones. A legacy is etched
into the minds of others and the stories they share about you.
                —Shannon Alder

In 2015, Arnold Palmer nominated Pat for inclusion in the prestigious World Golf Hall of Fame, golf's highest honor. Located near St. Augustine Florida, the Hall of Fame is supported by a consortium of twenty-six golf organizations around the world and is a rarity among athletic halls of fame in that it honors both men and women in a single site.

Unfortunately, the World Golf Hall of Fame has yet to accept Mr. Palmer's nomination and honor the world's greatest blind golfer with induction into their Hall. This is unfortunate in light of Pat's incredible accomplishments.

For the record, the most outstanding of those accomplishments bear listing in this one place.

Pat Browne Jr. won twenty-three USBGA National Championships between 1975 and 2005, winning twenty consecutively from 1978 to 1997.

He won twenty-four Corcoran Cup titles, sixteen consecutively, sponsored by the Guiding Eyes for the Blind. This tournament is considered to be the "Masters"

Here is Pat on the day a tournament trophy was named after him in Sarasota, Florida, 2016. With him from left to right is Gay Hardy, Sherry Browne, Kathy Stine, and Shannon Rainey. Pat is wearing a hat signed by Arnold Palmer, which another person bid on, won, and then gave to Pat. Palmer nominated Pat for the World Golf Hall of Fame.

of blind golf, so that the total of major championships Pat won is forty-seven. Jack Nicklaus won eighteen.

He recorded over seventy blind golf victories worldwide.

While playing blind golf tournaments and also serving as a world ambassador for blind golf, Pat helped raise millions for various charities for blind and other handicapped people, including providing guide dogs for the blind and vision-impaired.

He was the driving force behind establishing a World Cup blind golf competition between Great Britain and the United States, on setting the location for the Guiding Eyes Classic at Disney World and having the coaches' names appear on the Corcoran Cup Trophy alongside the golfers' names.

First hole at Royal County Down, Ireland, where Pat was a member and one of his favorite courses

The 18th hole at Cypress Point course in Pebble Beach, California, 2006, with wife Sherry, on vacation

Pat shot rounds of 75, 74, 79 and 75 at the Mission Hills Golf Club in Palm Springs, California, which stands as the lowest four consecutive rounds ever by a totally blind golfer.

He shot 80 at Pinehurst #2 in North Carolina.

He shot 85 in 1980 at the Old Course in St. Andrews, Scotland.

Pat shot 36 in 1982 on the back nine at Bryan Municipal Park Golf Course in Greensboro, North Carolina, which stands as the lowest nine-hole score in USBGA competition history.

He was the first blind golfer to record a hole-in-one at the historic 7th hole of the San Francisco Golf Club.

In 1990 Pat played a nine-hole exhibition with blindfolded U.S. Open Champion Payne Stewart and won by eighteen strokes.

Pat on the first hole of St. Andrews Old Course in Scotland, 2005

Perfect swing at St. Andrews

In 1988 the Golf Writers Association of America named him the Ben Hogan Award Winner, given annually to an individual who has continued to be active in golf despite a physical handicap or serious illness.

In 2007 the Metropolitan Golf Writers Association named Pat the Mary Bea Porter Award Winner, which recognizes an individual in golf who, through a heroic or humanitarian act, greatly enhances the lives of others.

He served as president of the USBGA from 1974 to 1992; was elected to the Tulane University Athletic Hall of Fame in 1983; was elected to the Sugar Bowl Athletic Hall of Fame in 1995; and was elected to the Louisiana Sports Hall of Fame in 1998.

Certainly, there could never be a more qualified

Pat receiving the Mary B. Porter Award in 2007 with PGA Tour Pro Ernie Els at the table, far right

candidate for induction into the World Golf Hall of Fame than Pat Browne Jr. as the inimitable Arnold Palmer well knew.

But world class accomplishments aside, time eventually catches up to all the great champions. Pat's days of championship golf were behind him after his final victory at the Guiding Eyes Classic in 2012 with Patrick as his coach.

He had retired from the Hibernia Bank in 2014 at the age of 80, having served as a trial attorney and bank president for forty years after he was blinded in the 1966 automobile crash.

He endured extensive congestive heart failure problems in 2015 and 2016 but bounced back from those as he had recovered from difficulties throughout his life. But in 2017 he finally faced the first challenge that he might not be able to overcome.

In many ways, the year 2017 was a challenging one for many of Pat's countrymen. Hurricane Harvey lashed Houston, Texas and western Louisiana causing death and destruction on a terrible scale. Mass shootings rocked Las Vegas and Sutherland Springs, Texas, while America and the world suffered numerous terrorist and bombing attacks. Americans needed a hero, the kind who selflessly put others first, looked out for those less fortunate than himself, and who graciously gave credit to others whenever it was due.

But that year a most heroic gentleman in New Orleans, Louisiana, was struggling with congestive heart failure, a disease that had steadily worsened during the preceding four years.

"I checked on him daily," Patrick said, "but that year

Pat and his son Patrick at the 2012 Guiding Eyes Tournament, the "Masters" of Blind Golf, after winning the Corcoran Cup

he required twenty-four-seven care from Mom and a private nurse through the night."

"He had been battling the heart problems for five years," Sherry recalled, "but that year he began retaining fluid, and endured more swelling than before."

The end came on the early morning of April 20, 2017, when Pat died peacefully in his sleep. "I had been with him the days before," Sherry said, "but he told me he wanted me to go to Mobile and visit my friends there for a brief respite. He said he was doing better and his swelling was down, and that I should be with my friends for an evening. I went to Mobile, and the next morning I got a call at 5 a.m., with the news that he had died. I believe he planned it that way, for me to be apart from him so I wouldn't have to go through his passing. That was so very like him, always thinking of others, lessening their pain in any way he could. I loved him so much!"

"It's very hard to see your hero failing," Patrick said, "but I didn't want that to stop us from leaving anything unsaid. I wanted him to know how I felt about him. I told Dad that he had always been my hero. The day before he died I was with him, and we knew it was coming. Before I left I gave him a hug and kiss, and told him how much he meant to me. That was the last time I saw him.

"The next day I got a call at 5 a.m. from the nurse saying that he was not breathing. I called 911 and rushed over there. The ambulance was at his home and was taking him to the hospital. They broke the news to me in the waiting room. It was such a blessing to me that I had had closure with him, and he knew how I felt. He had talked about how the Lord had blessed him with three daughters, then blessed him again with a son, all of whom he loved so very much.

"Then he told me that I had been his best friend, just as he and his dad had been. Looking back on it I'm very thankful that we spent so much time together, with Sherry as a family, and then with him playing golf. He said he had hoped to pass the game along to me as his dad had passed it on to him. I told him how glad I was that he did.

"Those last two days were very difficult," Patrick said, "but I wouldn't trade them for anything. It was wonderful leaving nothing unsaid between us."

Patrick "Pat" Walsh Browne Jr. died peacefully in his sleep on April 20, 2017, at the age of 84. His family, including Sherry and his four children, and nine grandchildren, and a multitude of friends celebrated his life at a Funeral Mass at Holy Name of Jesus Catholic Church on St. Charles Avenue, at noon on April 25. He was interred wearing his Louisiana Club tie and his New Orleans Country Club championship jacket.

Of the numerous tributes paid to him by fellow attorneys, secretaries, friends and acquaintances, perhaps one of the most appropriate was given by Natalia Gonzales, the executive director of WRBH radio. "He was kind, smart, a true gentleman," she said, "who, despite his accident, made his life one of service and dedication to those in our community. I will miss his gentle humor and his unfailing support of WRBH."

David Clark eulogized him saying he was the greatest man in the world.

But it was Patrick's son and Pat's grandson, Patrick IV, who may have had the very best last word. Upon hearing that his grandfather had passed away, he said, "Now Granddad can see how beautiful Sherry is."

INDEX